As You Like It Cookbook

As You Like It Cookbook

Imaginative Gourmet Dishes With Exciting Vegetarian Options

RON PICKARSKI

SQUAREONE
PUBLISHERS

Cover Designer: Phaedra Mastrocola
Cover Illustrator: Kathe Cobb
Text Illustrator: Kathe Cobb
Photographer: Michael Pizzuto
Photo Food Stylist: Ron Pickarski
Typesetter: Gary A. Rosenberg
In-house Editor: Marie Caratozzolo

Square One Publishers
Garden City Park, NY 11040
(516) 535–2010
www.squareonepublishers.com

Library of Congress Publisher's Cataloging-in-Publication Data

Pickarski, Ron.
    As you like it cookbook : imaginative gourmet dishes with exciting vegetarian options / Ron Pickarski.
  p. cm.
    Includes index.
    ISBN 0-7570-0013-4

    1. Vegetarian Cookery. I. Title.

    TX837 .P5274 2001
    641.5′636—dc21   00-012795

Printed in the United States of America

10   9   8   7   6   5   4   3   2   1

Contents

To my wife, Nancy Loving

Acknowledgments

Creating this cookbook has been a labor of love that was realized through the artistic efforts and expertise of a number of individuals. It is with the understanding of this team effort that I must give special thanks, from the deepest recesses of my heart, to a number of "artists" who have directly influenced this book.

First, I would like to extend a sincere thank-you to Rudy Shur, publisher of Square One, for taking on this project and for giving the *As You Like It Cookbook* its superb title; and to my editor, Marie Caratozzolo, for an excellent job of organizing and editing the material. I would also like to thank Sal Glynn, for his preliminary editing of the original manu-script. For their many hours of helping me kitchen-test the recipes, I must gratefully acknowledge Judith Lynn and Leslie Justus. My sincere appreciation is offered to Fred Arnal for his expert and very helpful marketing advice, and to photographer Michael Pizzutto for his outstanding photographs, which appear throughout this book. I must also extend my gratitude to the many fine cooking instructors who have nurtured me on my culinary journey. Finally, a very heart-felt thank-you goes to my wife and best friend, Nancy Loving, for her superb objective analysis in taste testing the nonvegetarian recipes, and for her unwavering support of my efforts.

Introduction

"Dressing on the side, please." "Can you leave out the onions?" "I'd like it medium-rare." "Can I get that with feta instead of goat cheese?" "Please use very little oil." "No anchovies!"

When it comes to food, we certainly like to have it our way. And why not? Eating is one of life's true pleasures; one that is central to our existence. It is also an area in which we are able to make choices that cater to our individual needs. With today's expanding global community and the fusion of ethnic cuisines, there is a constant variety of new and interesting items on the menu from which to choose. Food options and preferences are always changing, always evolving.

Since the 1970s, the United States has seen an increased interest in plant-based cuisine. For instance, products made from soybeans, such as tofu, soy milk, and soy cheese, once found only in health food stores, have made their way onto the shelves of most major supermarkets. Vegetables, too, have been elevated to a status never before seen. Modern growing techniques, transportation systems, and preservation methods have allowed fresh produce to make its way into kitchens throughout the country. And cooking methods, such as steaming and stir-frying, have made fresh vegetables more interesting and palatable than ever before. Gone, thank goodness, are the days when fresh broccoli florets or crisp green beans were boiled beyond recognition, and then dumped onto dinner plates in a limp, tasteless mass.

Of course, there are still plenty of people who choose not to give up their favorite meat or poultry dishes, or part with their beloved seafood recipes. Many, however, are beginning to incorporate more vegetarian-style dishes into their diets. Consequently, it has become increasingly challenging to prepare meals that cater to meat- and nonmeat-eaters alike.

But why are increasing numbers of people altering their diets to accommodate more meatless meals? Nutrition is probably the number one reason. With increased awareness of the health risks associated with overconsumption of meat—saturated fat in particular—nutrient-rich fresh produce, as well as whole grains and legumes, are attractive alternatives. But good health certainly isn't the only incentive for this nonmeat dietary lifestyle. Take the cost factor, for instance. Vegetarian proteins, such as beans and legumes, are an inexpensive option to high-priced meats. There are also ethical concerns—those who do not believe in the killing and suffering of animals opt for plant-based diets. And certain religious denominations, driven by the desire to live in harmony with nature and all living beings, do not believe that killing should be involved in any diet. Others simply choose to eat this way because they enjoy the taste, texture, and appealing colors that are characteristic of vegetables and grains.

There was a time when the term vegetarian simply referred to a person who avoided meat. Today, while vegetarians still eliminate red meat from their diets, they follow different dietary guidelines and fall into a number of categories—lacto, ovo, lacto-ovo, nouveau, and vegan. In addition to diets that include fruits, vegetables, legumes, and grains, *lacto vegetarians* eat dairy products but do not eat eggs; *ovo vegetarians* eat eggs but avoid dairy products; and *lacto-ovo vegetarians* eat both eggs and dairy products. *Vegans* eat only plant-based foods, while *nouveau vegetarians* avoid red meat, but eat fish and chicken, as well as dairy and eggs. Just on the outskirts of this vegetarian lifestyle are those who are considered *flexitarians*. Although primarily fruit, vegetable, and grain eaters, flexitarians also eat some eggs and dairy, and occasionally red meat, fish, and poultry.

The *As You Like It Cookbook* is an attempt to address these varied and ever-changing dietary preferences—no matter what the reason. The book opens with an introductory chapter that serves as a primer. It is the place to turn for basic information on the techniques, utensils, and ingredients called for in the book's recipes. It also includes listings of commonly used and readily available meat, egg, and dairy alternatives. This opening chapter is followed by nine more that offer over 150 easy-to-follow recipes for dishes that appeal to a broad range of tastes. There are sensational soups and salads and satisfying vegetarian entrées, as well as traditional fare that includes meat, poultry, and seafood. Show-stopping side dishes, condiments, sauces, and blue-ribbon desserts are included, plus much more. Rounding out the book is a Resource section that lists recommended brands and companies that make high-quality products.

In an effort to cater to the many different eating styles, the majority of recipes presented in this book offer simple ingredient adjustments that result in dishes that appeal to everyone. Most of the vegetarian dishes present alternatives for meat eaters. Conversely, recipes that include meat, poultry, or fish offer nonmeat ingredient options. Furthermore, if the recipe includes eggs and/or dairy products, a vegan alternative is given for those who follow a strictly plant-based diet.

If you are used to cooking only traditional meals and are new at preparing vegetarian-style dishes, you may feel somewhat intimidated and unsure of how to begin. After all, you may have never heard of—let alone used—products such as seitan or TVP. And although you may have tried tofu once or twice, you may have no idea that it is available in so many forms. Don't worry. Familiarizing yourself with these ingredients is easier than you may think. The increased popularity of eating less meat has caused the expansion of vegetarian and natural foods sections in many mainstream grocery stores. If you are new at the vegetarian game, this is certainly a good place to begin familiarizing yourself with these ingredients. Health food stores will give you an even greater product choice. Plus natural foods markets are opening up throughout the country. Take a trip to one of these stores and you will be amazed at the variety of foods that are on the shelves. While your local grocery store may carry one or two brands and types of soy milk,

for instance, a natural foods market is likely to carry dozens in a variety of flavors. It is astounding how much is actually out there and so readily available.

With one or two ingredient substitutions, this book will show you how easy it is to transform satisfying meat dishes into delectable meatless fare, and vegetarian dishes into meat-lover's choices. It will guide you in making meals that are gratifying and delicious, and cooked exactly "as you (and your family) like them."

1

Getting Started

As you learned in the Introduction, this cookbook is all about choices. It is about taking a recipe and preparing it "as you like it"—whether you're cooking for the meat-eaters in your family, or for those who prefer vegetarian cuisine (either lacto-ovo or vegan). A few ingredient adjustments can turn a traditional dish into a vegetarian masterpiece.

On your culinary journey, you may run across an unfamiliar term or ingredient, especially if you are used to traditional cooking and not well-versed in vegetarian alternatives. This is the place to turn for an explanation. Consider this chapter a primer—a place that provides a basic understanding of the equipment, techniques, and ingredients you will need to prepare the wide range of delicious dishes presented in the following chapters.

THE FIVE PS

Whenever I cook, I always keep the following motto—which I call the Five Ps—in mind: *Proper preparation prevents poor performance.* If you are properly prepared, the cooking process will be fast, easy, and enjoyable. It is the way the kitchen in a classical French restaurant operates. For instance, in French cuisine, four "mother sauces" serve as the basis for all others. They are made in relatively large quantities, and, during the course of the day, are used as needed. The cooks dip into these pots, taking out only as much of the "mother sauce" that is needed to create a new sauce.

Although I certainly don't expect you to maintain four simmering pots of sauce in your kitchen on any given day, there are a number of other ways in which you can maintain maximum cooking efficiency. The following suggestions will give you a few ideas.

❏ Have a well-stocked pantry that includes nonperishable items such as canned beans, dry pasta and grains, and regularly used herbs and spices. (See Stocking Your Pantry on page 7.)

❏ Keep certain perishable items on hand. Milk, eggs, fresh vegetables, and fruits, for instance, have a fairly long life when properly stored in the refrigerator.

❏ Arm yourself with the proper cooking utensils. Having the right type of knife, or the appropriate size pan or skillet can make food preparation a breeze.

❏ Keep good-quality frozen vegetables on hand, as well as frozen containers of sauces and broths. You can defrost these items for use at a moment's notice.

❏ Buy vegetarian meat alternatives or other prepared natural foods to store in your freezer. Generally, they are dry or pre-cooked and freeze well.

❏ Whenever possible, plan your menu for the coming week, and shop for several days' worth of groceries at one time.

❏ When preparing foods that keep well, make extra. Then store the extra portion or portions in appropriate containers, and refrigerate or freeze them for use at a later time. Keep this in mind the next time you cook a pot of beans, for instance, or when you prepare a sauce or marinade. Most of the sauces in this book will keep for at least a week when properly stored and refrigerated. In the freezer, they will last for months.

Taking the time to follow these simple guidelines, which are designed to encourage cooking efficiency in the kitchen, will help make meal preparation both easy and enjoyable.

BASIC EQUIPMENT

Every cook knows that in addition to having a good recipe and the right ingredients, working with the proper equipment is just as important. The right tools can make cooking easy. In most cases, when setting up your kitchen with basic equipment, I recommend buying the best you can afford. Avoid cheap gadgets, opting instead for solid, dependable equipment that will last for years. I suggest equipping your kitchen with the following items.

BAKING SHEETS. Rectangular in shape, baking sheets—also called cookie sheets—come in a variety of sizes. Some have shallow sides, while others have none.

BLENDER. Ideal for mixing liquids, blenders are also excellent for puréeing and grinding foods. Although there are many good-quality blenders on the market, I recommend the Waring brand. It is a high-quality piece of equipment and is repairable (most blenders are not and must be scrapped if they break).

COFFEE GRINDER. A small inexpensive coffee grinder is ideal for pulverizing dried herbs and spices. Just be sure to use it for this purpose only, and to clean it well after each use.

COLANDER. Designed to drain fruits, vegetables, and pastas, these strainers range in size from small hand-held versions to large bowl-shaped types.

ELECTRIC MIXER. A large-capacity table mixer is invaluable for whipping potatoes and mixing cake batters. I recommend the KitchenAid brand, because it is a high-quality piece of equipment, and it has a variety of useful attachments. Small hand-held mixers are also great for smaller jobs, like whipping cream and blending sauces.

FOOD PROCESSOR. For chopping, mincing, and shredding foods, a food processor is invaluable for the busy cook. Because it has a large-capacity bowl, it is best suited for large

STOCKING YOUR PANTRY

A well-stocked pantry is a must for the good cook. Having some basic staple items at your fingertips will make it easier for you to whip a dish together at any given time. The following items, which are used throughout this book, are recommended. Keep them, along with any other regularly used nonperishables, on hand.

Basics

bases / bouillon
(regular and vegetarian beef
and chicken, and vegetable)
beans, dried (assorted)
bread crumbs
cornstarch or arrowroot
grains, dried (assorted)
pasta, dry
rice, brown and white
unbleached white flour
whole wheat flour
whole wheat pastry flour

Oils

canola oil
olive oil
peanut oil
sesame oil

Produce

carrots
garlic
onions
potatoes

Sweeteners

brown sugar
corn syrup
granulated sugar
honey

Vinegars

balsamic vinegar
cider vinegar
red wine vinegar
white wine vinegar

Dried Seasonings

basil
bay leaves
black pepper
caraway seeds
cinnamon, ground
cumin, ground
fennel seeds
garlic powder
ginger, ground
mustard, dry
nutmeg, ground
onion powder
oregano
rosemary
sea salt
tarragon
thyme

Flavorings

almond extract
lemon juice
maple syrup
mirin
vanilla extract

Wines

red wine
white wine

Dairy & Dairy Substitutes

butter
coconut milk
eggs
milk
soy milk

Condiments

mayonnaise (regular and soy)
miso (white and dark)
mustard (yellow and Dijon-style)
soy sauce
(tamari or other type)

Canned Items

broth
(chicken, beef, vegetable)
legumes, assorted
tomato sauce
tomatoes, whole

Miscellaneous

agar powder
flax meal
flaxseeds

amounts. Some models come with small-capacity attachments for small jobs.

KNIVES. Good-quality knives are necessary items in any kitchen. Without them, you may find yourself mashing food instead of slicing it. The most useful knife is the French chef's knife, which is used for cutting and chopping most foods. A good paring knife, a boning knife, and a serrated knife that easily cuts bread are also essential. And be sure to have a good knife sharpener to maintain the blades.

MIXING BOWLS. Ranging in size from small to very large, mixing bowls are made of glass, plastic, and metal.

POTS AND PANS. Every good kitchen should have at least one 10-inch and 12-inch sauté pan or skillet, as well as 1-, 2-, and 4-quart saucepans/pots with covers. A large stockpot or soup pot is also important. Select cookware that has at least a twenty-five-year warranty. I recommend the Swiss-made Kuhn-Rikon brand.

PRESSURE COOKER. A pressure cooker is a great piece of equipment for preparing soups, stews, vegetables, beans, and grains in a matter of minutes.

STEAMER BASKET. Perfect for steaming fresh vegetables and other foods, this vented metal basket has collapsible sides and fits inside pots of all sizes. The food is placed on top of the basket, which sits in the pot over boiling water.

WIRE WHISK. Ranging in size from very tiny to very large, wire whisks are perfect for blending sauces and whipping eggs.

WOK. This versatile piece of cookware is highly recommended. A wok is so deep that it allows you to toss large amounts of ingredients quickly—without tossing them out of the pot! And because the bottom of the wok is fairly narrow, you can also cook small amounts of food with equally good results.

GLOSSARY OF INGREDIENTS

The following ingredients are called for in recipes throughout this book. They are briefly defined and listed according to categories.

Oils

Oil plays an important role in good cooking. It is used to enhance the flavor of a dish, to help promote browning, and to prevent food from sticking. The following oils are used in moderation in *As You Like It* recipes.

CANOLA OIL. Mild in flavor, canola oil is a good choice for cooking and baking when a neutral-tasting oil is desired. As an added bonus, it has approximately 6 percent less saturated fat than other oils.

OLIVE OIL. The cornerstone of the Mediterranean diet for thousands of years, olive oil is one of the oldest culinary oils. The finest and most flavorful olive oil is the extra-virgin variety. It is produced by the first pressing of the olives and has a very low acid content of 1 percent. Olive oil becomes rancid easily, especially when exposed to heat or light, so always store it tightly sealed in a cool dark place.

SESAME OIL. Made from pressed sesame seeds, sesame oil, which is available in plain or roasted varieties, is strong flavored. Just a small amount can add a distinctive taste to foods. (Unless instructed, use only the plain variety for the recipes in this book.)

Vinegars

Vinegar's versatility has long been recognized. Since ancient times, it has been used as an antiseptic, a cleaning solution, and a medicine. In the kitchen, vinegar plays a vital role as a flavoring agent and a food preserver. And it can be made from anything that contains sugar or starch, particularly fruits, grains, and sugar. Depending on its origins, vinegar possesses distinctive flavor, color, and aroma.

BALSAMIC VINEGAR. Originally used as a disinfectant, balsamic vinegar is an aged reduction of Trebbiano grapes. It is aromatic and strong-flavored, and has a deep rich brown color. Balsamic vinegar is produced in the Modena and Reggio regions of Italy, where it is aged in fragrant wooden casks for a minimum of six years, although most varieties age for decades. The longer the vinegar ages, the mellower and more expensive it is.

RICE VINEGAR. Delicately flavored rice vinegar is made from rice wine, and has about half the level of acid as cider vinegar. Varieties that are derived from brown rice (labeled "brown rice vinegar") have greater nutritional integrity than varieties made from white rice, which often contain additives. Rice vinegar is widely available in natural foods stores, Asian markets, and many supermarkets. If a recipe calls for rice vinegar and only cider vinegar is on hand, mix the cider vinegar with equal parts of water, and use it in this diluted state.

WINE VINEGAR. Red and white wine vinegars, which come from grapes of the same color, are the two main types. The red wine variety is full-bodied, while the white is more delicate in flavor.

Herbs and Spices

Flavorful herbs and spices are great food enhancers. As a general rule, I recommend using fresh herbs whenever possible. However, most dried varieties can be used with equally good results. When figuring equivalents, keep in mind that 1 tablespoon of a fresh herb is equivalent to 1 teaspoon dried.

BASIL. Nothing compares in flavor and aroma to fresh basil. This sweet herb is powerful enough to enhance hearty dishes such as stews and beans, yet delicate enough to sprinkle on salads or slices of fresh tomatoes. Along with fresh garlic, cheese, and pine nuts, basil is the star ingredient in pesto sauces. Avoid dry basil, which has little flavor.

BAY LEAVES. Leaves from the evergreen bay laurel tree, bay leaves have a woodsy pungent flavor that enhances stews, soups, and a variety of meat and vegetable dishes. Use bay leaves sparingly—one leaf is strong enough to flavor an entire pot of soup or stew. And be sure to remove the leaves from the dish before serving.

CARAWAY SEEDS. Available whole or ground, flavorful caraway seeds add a licorice-flavored crunch to breads, cheeses, and vegetables. They are also used to flavor soups and stews.

CINNAMON. Made from the dried inner bark of the *Cinnamomum zeylanicum* tree, sweet aromatic cinnamon comes in many forms—powder, chips, and rolled sticks. It is often used to flavor fruits, pies, and breads. As cinnamon loses its intensity after a few months, it should be purchased in small amounts.

CUMIN. A slightly bitter and pungent spice, cumin was once found only in Middle Eastern cuisine. Now it is more commonly used to give added dimension to fish and lamb, as well as vegetable and grain dishes and salad dressings.

FENNEL SEEDS. These oval, greenish-brown seeds from the fennel plant have a slight licorice flavor. Used in both their whole and powdered forms, fennel seeds are commonly added to breads, and used to flavor soups, stews, and sauces.

HERBAMARE. A product of Switzerland, herbamare is a flavorful combination of herbs, spices, and salt.

MACE. An aromatic spice made from the bright red covering of the nutmeg kernel, mace is stronger flavored than nutmeg but used in the same way. Mace adds flavor to fruit desserts, spice cakes, and cookies, as well as some vegetable dishes, particularly those with carrots.

OREGANO. Commonly used in both fresh and dried forms, oregano is a pungent herb of the mint family. Its robust flavor is decidedly Mediterranean, and it is commonly used in Italian and Greek cuisines to flavor tomato sauces, soups, and stews. It also adds spark to salads and dressings, and is a favorite with seafood and poultry.

ROSEMARY. An extremely pungent herb with a fresh piney odor, rosemary is a member of the mint family. Commonly, its silver-green needle-shaped leaves are used fresh or dried to flavor meats (especially lamb), sauces, and potatoes.

SAVORY. Closely related to the mint family, savory has a peppery, aromatic, slightly pungent taste. It is used to flavor soups, meats, and poultry dishes, as well as legumes, sauces, stuffings, and vegetables. Savory is strong flavored and should be used sparingly.

SEA SALT. Obtained from evaporated sea water, granular sea salt contains trace minerals that are lacking in regular salt.

TARRAGON. Narrow, pointed dark green tarragon leaves are often seen floating inside bottles of gourmet vinegar. Tarragon has a mild, delicate licorice flavor, and is a popular addition to egg and seafood dishes, salads, and sauces.

THYME. Pungent with a minty-lemon flavor, thyme is commonly used in breads, omelets, stuffings, stews, and soups. Vegetable dishes, particularly potatoes, mushrooms, squash, and eggplant, can benefit from just a pinch of thyme. And rubbing thyme over poultry, roasts, and fish before cooking will impart its unique flavor.

Condiments and Flavorings

The following ingredients, which are readily available in most grocery stores, health food stores, and gourmet shops, can add a range of flavors to a variety of dishes.

BASE. Vegetable, chicken, and beef bases are reduced soups, usually in paste form. They are similar to bouillon, only richer and not quite as salty. Bases are found in the soup section of most supermarkets. They come in jars and must be refrigerated once opened. Vogue Vege Base is a dry soup stock that comes in vegetarian onion and vegetable flavors. Highly recommended, this base is a natural product that contains no chemicals or additives, and is very low in sodium compared to others.

BOUILLON. Bouillon cubes or granules are added to water to provide an instant beef-, chicken-, or vegetable-flavored base for soups and sauces. Most commercial varieties are very high in sodium, although reduced-sodium varieties are becoming more available. Harvest Direct has a vegetarian line of powdered stocks that are vegetable, beef, ham, and chicken flavored.

MUSTARD. A pungent condiment used to flavor foods, sauces, and marinades, mustard falls into two general categories—dry and prepared. Dry mustard is the concentrated powder from the crushed seeds of the mustard plant. Prepared varieties can be light or dark, depending on the color of the seeds used. Mild yellow mustard, also called American

FOOD PREPARATION
AND COOKING TECHNIQUES

Successful dishes must include two integral components—great recipes and high-quality ingredients. However, proper food preparation and accurate cooking methods are equally important to gratifying cuisine, as they help develop a food's flavor and enhance its texture and appearance. The following basic cooking terms and techniques will be helpful to you as you prepare the recipes found in this book.

Al dente. A term describing pasta, rice, or vegetables that are cooked to the point of tenderness while still remaining firm "to the bite."

Boil. To heat liquid to a temperature at which bubbles appear on the surface.

Butterfly. To split poultry, meat, or fish down the center, carefully cutting almost, but not completely through. The two halves are then opened flat to resemble a butterfly.

Caramelize. To sauté, roast, or grill fruits or vegetables until their natural sugars break down, giving them an intensely sweet flavor and golden glaze.

Chop. To cut food into irregularly shaped pieces.

Dice. To cut food into small cubes. Finely diced foods are cut into $1/8$-inch cubes. Larger diced foods are cut into $3/4$- to 1-inch cubes.

Dredge. To lightly coat food with flour, bread crumbs, or sugar, immediately before cooking.

Flake. To shave or thinly slice food about $1/8$-inch thick.

Grate. To grind or shred food into fine particles using a hand grater or food processor.

Grill. To cook food quickly over high heat on either an indoor or outdoor barbecue grill.

Julienne. To cut vegetables, meat, or cheese into matchstick-sized pieces.

Marinate. To soak food in a seasoned liquid before cooking.

Mince. To chop food into very fine pieces.

Poach. To gently simmer food, usually fish, poultry, or eggs, that is partially covered in water or a seasoned liquid.

Reduce. To boil a liquid until it has partially evaporated, resulting in a richer, more concentrated liquid.

Roast. To cook food in an oven or other enclosed dry-heat environment.

Sauté. To cook food lightly in an open pan.

Shred. To cut food into very thin strips.

Simmer. To gently cook liquid just at or below the boiling point.

Steam. To cook food in a vented container over boiling water.

Stir-fry. To cook food quickly over high heat, while stirring constantly.

Whip. To beat food, generally eggs or cream, with a wire whisk, electric mixer, or fork until fluffy.

mustard, is a blend of white mustard seeds, sugar, and vinegar. Dijon mustard, which originated in Dijon, France, is a sharp-tasting, smooth-textured condiment made with brown mustard seeds, white wine, and seasonings.

MIRIN. Used as a flavoring agent, mirin is a sweet wine that is made from sweet rice, rice koji (a natural rice culture), and water. Made with or without sea salt, mirin has a low alcohol content that evaporates quickly when heated. The variety with salt is used in savory foods, while the unsalted variety is appropriate for sweet dishes. Mirin is used to flavor sauces, salad dressings, soups, and desserts. MCOA brand is recommended.

MISO. A fermented paste made from soybeans, grains, and salt, miso has been a staple seasoning in Japan for thousands of years. Miso is used mainly as a flavoring agent for soups, sauces, and marinades, and comes in a wide range of flavors, depending on the bean or grain from which it is made. Light-colored white and yellow misos are delicate-flavored and typically used in cream sauces, light soups, sweet vegetables, and salad dressings. Examples of dark-colored varieties include barley miso, brown rice miso, and hatcho miso (made from soybeans). Darker in color and stronger flavored than light misos, they are typically used in hearty winter soups and stews.

TAMARI SOY SAUCE. This traditional Japanese soy sauce, which was originally the rich dark liquid that pooled on the surface of fermenting miso, is naturally made from soybeans, water, and sea salt. Because its flavor stands up under high heat, tamari is a good choice for dishes that range from soups and sauces to stir-fries and stews.

Vegetables

The following fresh vegetables are called for in a number of recipes in this book. Most are fairly perishable and should be purchased shortly before using. When not used immediately, be sure to store them properly in the refrigerator for maximum shelf life.

BELL PEPPERS. Once available only in green varieties, bell peppers are now found in red, purple, yellow, and orange. The red types are actually green peppers that have been allowed to mature and ripen on the vine. They are softer and sweeter than the green ones. Generally, the other colored bell peppers, which were once grown only in Holland, are now grown in the United States as well. They are also sweeter and milder than the green varieties. (For roasting instructions, see the inset on page 71.)

BOK CHOY. Sweet and crisp, bok choy is a Chinese vegetable that is similar in appearance to celery. Its long stalks are topped with dark green leaves. The stalks are crisp like celery, but whiter, smoother, and without strings. Use bok choy in salads, stir-fries, or any dish in which you would use celery.

BURDOCK. Called *gobo* in Japan, the hardy burdock plant grows wild throughout the United States. Its long dark root resembles a carrot in shape and is a great addition to soups, stews, and casseroles.

CABBAGE, NAPA. Also called Chinese cabbage, Napa cabbage has pale green "leafy" leaves that are slightly sweet. It is often shredded and added to salads, although it is also enjoyed cooked, usually sautéed.

GREEN TOMATOES. Unripe tomatoes, green varieties are commonly pickled, added to soups, or made into relish. In the Southern United States, they are often sliced, dredged in flour, and fried.

LEEKS. Actually members of the lily family, these large onion-like vegetables have long, flat green leaves that taper to a white bulb. They have a sweet, mild onion taste. Leeks are typically filled with sand and dirt, and must be carefully rinsed clean before using.

PORTABELLA MUSHROOMS. Meaty and satisfying, these cultivated mushrooms have very large caps that are delicious roasted, sautéed, or grilled. They can be served in their entirety or thinly sliced and added to other dishes.

SCALLIONS. Also called *green onions,* scallions are immature onions that have not yet developed outer skins. They are sweet and mild tasting, and sold with their long green stalk-like leaves.

SHIITAKE MUSHROOMS. With their delicate yet woodsy flavor, Japanese shiitake mushrooms add gourmet flair to just about any dish. They have broad fleshy caps and tough stems that must be removed. Cooking greatly enhances their flavor. Shiitake are also called *Golden Oaks* or *Black Forests,* and they are available—both fresh and dried—in most supermarkets.

Sea Vegetables

Sea vegetables—plants that are harvested from the sea—are a relatively unknown alternative food in mainstream America. Virtually fat-free, vegetables of the sea are also low in calories and rich in vitamins and minerals, especially trace minerals that land vegetables lack due to demineralized soil. Available in most natural foods stores and Asian markets,

they are staple items in many vegetarian kitchens. If you are not familiar with sea vegetables, go easy with them at first. Start by including them in dishes in which they are not the main ingredients.

AGAR-AGAR. Used primarily as a thickener, agar-agar—also called *kanten* or simply *agar*—is derived from various species of red algae. It is rich in calcium, iron, phosphorus, and vitamins A, B-complex, C, D, and K. Agar is an excellent vegan substitute for gelatin, which is an animal product. It is nutritionally superior to gelatin, and sets at room temperature.

Agar is available in powder, flakes, and bars. Both flakes and bars can be dissolved in the simmering liquid of a recipe. Powder, on the other hand, must be dissolved in water that is either cold or room temperature before it is added to hot liquid. The correct proportion is 1 tablespoon flakes (or 1 teaspoon powder) to 1 cup water. Never try to dissolve agar in any liquid that contains oil, which will prevent the agar from dissolving. And when adding raw citrus juice or zest to any dish that contains agar, do so only after the agar dissolves. The citrus will break down the agar, destroying its gelling capabilities.

ARAME. After this sweet, delicate-flavored sea vegetable is harvested, it is shredded into thin strips and dried. To rehydrate, it needs to be soaked in hot water for 5 minutes. Arame can be tossed into salads, incorporated in soups and stews, or added to sautéed vegetables for additional color, flavor, and nutrition.

DULSE. A member of the red algae family, mild-tasting dulse can be eaten raw or toasted. It was once enjoyed as a snack-like chip in Western Europe and New England. Found in the waters of the North Atlantic and the

Pacific Northwest, dulse is a great addition to salads, cooked vegetables, and grain dishes (I love it in my breakfast porridge). You can use dulse in any recipe that calls for wakame.

KOMBU. One of the most versatile sea vegetables, kombu is a good source of calcium, sugar, potassium, iodine, and vitamin A, and has appreciable amounts of the B-complexes and glutamic acid. Sold dried in flat sheets or strips that measure seven to eight inches, kombu is used most commonly as a flavoring agent. Small pieces may be added to a pot of cooking beans or to seitan dishes for improved flavor and digestibility. Kombu is also a common flavor enhancer for miso and other soups. Once cooked, it is taken out of the soup, thinly sliced, and then returned to the pot.

NORI. Rich in calcium, iron, and vitamins A, B, and C, nori is a popular sea vegetable that has been dried and pressed into thin sheets. Ranging in color from deep green to purplish black, nori sheets are a common sight in Japanese sushi bars, where they are used as wrappers for various fish and vegetable rolls.

WAKAME. Wakame is a long, thin sea vegetable that is very popular in Japan. In addition to adding flavor and nutrition to food, it also helps soften the tough fibers of other vegetables as they cook. Wakame's sweet taste and delicate texture make it an especially welcome ingredient in soups. When dried wakame is rehydrated, it resembles slippery spinach with a thick rib down the middle. This vegetable of the sea is also a wonderful complement to onion, noodle, and grain dishes.

Grains and Flours

Grains are actually the seeds of cultivated grasses. Along with beans, they have been considered staple foods in many countries for thousands of years. Whole grains and the flours made from them are nutritionally superior to refined grains and flours. For additional information on cooking whole grains, refer to the inset on page 15.

ARBORIO RICE. An Italian grain from Northern Italy, Arborio rice is stubby, thick, and very starchy. It absorbs flavor as it cooks yet maintains a firm and chewy texture, making it the perfect rice for risotto. Its high-starch kernels result in a creamy texture.

BASMATI RICE. Basmati is a long-grained fragrant rice with a nutty flavor, and is popular in many Middle Eastern and Indian dishes. Basmati's literal translation is "queen of fragrance."

BARLEY. In its many forms, barley is a hardy grain that is used in dishes ranging from cereals and breads to soups and side dishes. Its most nutritious form is the hulled variety in which only the outer husk is removed. When barley is processed into *pearl barley,* its hull is removed and the inner kernel is polished. Pearl barley, which has a distinctive nutty taste, takes about forty-five minutes to cook. A quick-cooking variety, which is ready in about ten minutes, is also available.

BROWN RICE. Nutty in flavor and texture, brown rice comes in short-, medium-, and long-grain varieties. It is the whole unpolished grain, and is brown in color because it retains the outer layer of bran. Brown rice is rich in fiber, protein, calcium, vitamin E, and most of the B vitamins.

BULGHUR. Whole wheat berries that have been steamed, cracked, and then dried, bulghur (or bulgur) has its origins in the Middle East. To cook this light nutty-flavored grain, simply

THE GOODNESS OF GRAINS

Whole grains are certainly nutritious—they are low in fat, cholesterol-free, rich in fiber, and packed with vitamins and minerals. In all of their wholesome nutty goodness, grains make satisfying pilafs and side dishes. They are also added to stuffings, cookies, breads, and salads, and some varieties are used as breakfast cereals. Whole grains are available in natural foods stores, although many grocery stores stock the more common varieties, such as brown rice, bulghur wheat, oats, and barley.

The chart below provides the cooking requirements for popular whole grains. It lists the amount of water needed to cook 1 cup of each grain, as well as the cooking time, directions, and yield information.

Cooking Chart for Grains

For most grains, the following **basic cooking directions** apply: Bring the water to boil in a saucepan, and add the grain. Stir once, reduce the heat to low, and simmer covered for the required time. Do not stir the grain as it cooks, or it will become a sticky mass. Once cooked, let the grain sit for about 5 minutes before fluffing with a fork and serving.

GRAIN (1 CUP)	WATER	COOKING TIME	DIRECTIONS	YIELD
Barley, pearled	2 cups	50 to 60 minutes.	Basic cooking directions above.	3½ cups
Brown rice, long-grain	2 cups	45 to 60 minutes	Basic cooking directions above.	3 cups
Brown rice, short-grain	2 cups	45 to 50 minutes	Basic cooking directions above.	3½ cups
Cornmeal, coarse	4 cups, lukewarm	25 to 45 minutes	Add water, stir, cover, and let stand.	3 cups
Couscous	2 cups	5 to 10 minutes	Add water, stir, cover, and let stand.	4 cups
Millet	3 cups	20 to 30 minutes	Basic cooking directions above.	4½ cups
Oats, quick-cooking	1¾ cups	1 minute	Basic cooking directions above.	2 cups
Oats, rolled	2 cups	5 to 20 minutes	Basic cooking directions above, but stir occasionally.	2 cups
Quinoa	2 cups	10 to 15 minutes	Basic cooking directions above.	2½ cups
Rye, cracked	2½ cups	15 to 20 minutes.	Basic cooking directions above, but stir occasionally.	3 cups
Rye, whole berries	2½ cups	1 to 1½ hours	Basic cooking directions above.	3 cups
Wheat, bulghur (precooked)	2 cups	30 to 45 minutes	Pour boiling water over wheat in a heatproof bowl. Stir, cover, and let sit until most water is absorbed. Drain.	2½ cups
Wheat, cracked	2 cups	15 to 25 minutes	Basic cooking directions above.	2½ cups
Wheat, rolled	2 cups	20 to 30 minutes	Basic cooking directions above, but stir occasionally.	2½ cups
Wild rice	3 cups	50 to 60 minutes	Basic cooking directions above.	4¼ cups

cover it with boiling water and let stand for a few hours or until tender.

CORNMEAL. This fine-grain meal is made from ground degermed corn, and is versatile enough to be used in both sweet and savory dishes. Cornmeal is the starring ingredient in polenta and cornbreads, and is either yellow, white, or blue in color, depending on the type of corn used.

COUSCOUS. Couscous is actually a pasta that has been formed into tiny grains. Most varieties are made with refined durum wheat, although whole wheat varieties are also available. Couscous is often called *Moroccan pasta.*

GLUTEN FLOUR. Gluten flour is pure gluten (an elastic protein) that has been extracted from grains, particularly wheat.

MILLET. Tiny mild-flavored millet grains can be used in place of rice in most dishes. Millet is a staple item in the cuisines of Africa and Asia.

QUINOA. Pronounced *keen•wah,* this quick-cooking grain is mild flavored and wheat free. It can be enjoyed plain as a cereal, or used as an ingredient in puddings, pilafs, and stews.

WHOLE WHEAT FLOUR. Made from ground whole wheat kernels, whole wheat flour contains the grain's nutrient-rich bran and germ. It is nutritionally superior to white flour.

WHOLE WHEAT PASTRY FLOUR. Compared to regular whole wheat flour, this pastry flour is better for baked goods. It is made from softer, more finely ground wheat, and produces lighter, softer quick breads, muffins, and other baked items.

WILD RICE. Actually a North American aquatic grass, wild rice is available in short-, medium-, and long-grain varieties. It is dark brown in color and has a nutty flavor.

Legumes

Rich in fiber and protein, low-fat legumes are mainstays of a vegetarian diet. For preparation and cooking instructions for dried legumes, refer to the inset on pages 18 and 19.

AZUKI BEANS. Also spelled *aduki* and *adzuki,* these tiny reddish-brown beans are sweet-flavored and commonly used in the cuisines of China and Japan.

BLACK BEANS. Also called *turtle beans,* kidney-shaped black beans are staples in the cuisines of Cuba and South America. They are slightly mealy in texture and have a prominent flavor that makes them a delicious addition to stews, soups, and chilis. Black beans are also commonly served over rice.

BLACK-EYED PEAS. Sometimes called *cowpeas,* black-eyed peas are small and oval in shape. They are slightly sweet and popular in Creole and Cajun-style dishes, as well as ethnic foods of America's Southland.

CANNELLINI BEANS. Especially popular in Italian-style dishes, creamy white cannellini beans are shaped like small kidney beans.

CHICKPEAS. Also called *garbanzo beans,* nutty-flavored chickpeas are round, tan-colored legumes that hail from the Mediterranean area of the Middle East. They can be ground into paste and used in dips and sauces, or tossed into soups, stews, or salads. The whole dried bean can also be ground into flour.

KIDNEY BEANS. Medium-sized legumes with dark red skin and cream-colored flesh, kidney beans are firm and somewhat mealy-textured. This bean's full-bodied flavor is a popular addition to rice dishes and chili.

LENTILS. These small flat seeds from the *Lens*

culinaris plant are staples in Indian cuisine. Popular in the United States as well, lentils are commonly used in soups and stews, as well as burgers and meatless loaves. They do not require soaking before cooking.

LIMA BEANS. Fresh and dried lima beans come in a variety of sizes and colors. The fresh beans are traditionally served as simple side dishes, while the dried varieties are commonly added to soups, stews, and casseroles.

NAVY BEANS. A type of white bean, navy beans are popular additions to salads, pastas, and soups.

PINTO BEANS. Small kidney-shaped pinto beans are beige in color with brownish-red spots. They are similar in flavor to kidney beans, and are popular in both Indian and Caribbean-style dishes.

SPLIT PEAS. These tiny peas are actually dried beans without the skin. Flat and smooth on one side, split peas are most commonly cooked with water and seasonings to make split pea soup. Like lentils, they do not require soaking before cooking.

SOYBEANS. An outstanding source of protein, soybeans have been a principal crop of Eastern Asia for thousands of years. A versatile legume, it is the source of a variety of traditional natural foods, including miso, soy milk, soy sauce, tempeh, tofu, and soy oil.

Sweeteners

Although granulated white sugar and honey are called for in a number of recipes in this book, a variety of "sweet" options are available as well. Depending on your taste and nutritional preferences, feel free to substitute one of the following sweeteners for another.

However, to maintain similar measurements, replace liquid sweeteners with other liquid types, and granulated sugars with other granulated varieties.

BARLEY MALT SYRUP. This sweetener is made from sprouted whole barley. It has a caramel flavor and is about half as sweet as sugar or honey. Barley malt syrup is high in carbohydrates and contains some vitamins and minerals. It is also the least expensive of the natural sweeteners. This syrup must be stored in a sanitary jar and kept in a cool, dry place. If it begins to ferment, heating the syrup will kill the active enzymes. Barley malt syrup that is blended with corn syrup is not as desirable as the pure barley malt variety.

BROWN SUGAR. Brown sugar is refined white sugar to which molasses has been added.

HONEY. The sweetest of the liquid sweeteners, honey is about 20 to 30 percent sweeter than granulated sugar. When using honey as a sugar substitute, use half the amount called for.

POWDERED SUGAR. Also called *confectioner's sugar*, powdered sugar is granulated sugar that has been pulverized to a fine powder. It also contains a small percentage of cornstarch, which prevents it from caking.

RICE SYRUP. This cultured (fermented) syrup is light and delicate and about half as sweet as sugar. It is made by converting the starch found in rice into sugar. Used in combination with other sweeteners, such as Sucanat or honey, it helps neutralize their dominant flavor. Syrups made with brown rice are darker in color than those made from white rice, but the flavor is the same. This sweetener is also available in powdered form.

SUCANAT. Derived from the term *"sugar cane*

PREPARING DRIED BEANS

Fresh beans or legumes, which differ in size, appearance, and flavor, contain excessive moisture, which results in a short shelf life. Consequently, many beans are dried as a means of preservation.

Legumes fall into one of three major categories—hard, medium-soft, and soft. Soft varieties include black-eyed peas, lentils, and split peas. Medium-soft types include aduki, black, lima, navy, pinto, and turtle beans. Beans such as dark aduki, chickpeas, and soybeans fall under the hard-bean category. Depending on their type—hard, medium-soft, or soft—the necessary water amounts and cooking times for dried varieties will vary. However, there are some general preparation and cooking guidelines that are universal.

CLEANING

Packages of dried beans may contain shriveled or discolored beans, or empty shells. Always spread the dried beans out on a baking sheet or large plate and sort through them, discarding those that are blemished. Place the beans in a bowl, add enough water to cover, and swish them around. Discard any beans or shells that float to the top. Transfer the beans to a colander, and rinse well.

PRESOAKING

With the exception of certain dried legumes, such as lentils, split peas, and black-eyed peas, most varieties benefit from presoaking before they are cooked. First, soaking beans makes them more nutritious because it causes certain minerals, such as calcium, iron, and zinc, to become more available to the body. Second, soaking reduces gas-producing oligosaccharides. For this reason, never cook beans in their soaking water. Always rinse and drain them, and then cook them in a pot of fresh water. Finally, soaking greatly reduces a bean's cooking time.

Basically, there are two presoaking methods—slow soaking and quick soaking. Although both are effective, the slow method is preferred because it is better for reducing oligosaccharides.

Slow-Soaking Method

Once the beans are cleaned and rinsed, place them in a large pot or bowl. For every cup of beans, add four cups of cold water. Allow the beans to soak for a minimum of four hours and a maximum of twelve. If you are soaking for four hours, you can do so at room temperature. However, if you are soaking for a longer period, the beans may begin to ferment, so place them in the refrigerator.

Generally, hard-bean varieties require about six to eight hours soaking time, while medium-soft varieties usually need from two to four hours. As mentioned earlier, soft beans do not require any soaking.

Quick-Soaking Method

The quick method requires less soaking time, but a little more initial effort. After the beans are cleaned and rinsed, place them in a large pot. For every cup of beans, add four cups of water. Place the pot over high heat and bring to a boil. Reduce the heat to low, and simmer the beans for seven to ten minutes. Then cover the pot and turn off the heat. Let the beans soak for at least one hour, or half of the time that is required for that particular bean when slow soaking (see above).

natural," sucanat is a granulated sweetener that is obtained from evaporated sugar cane juice. Sucanat provides small amounts of calcium, iron, and vitamins A and C. Found in health food stores, Sucanat is similar to brown sugar, and can be used the same way.

COOKING

After rinsing the soaked beans, place them in a pot, along with the amount of fresh water recommended in the Cooking Dried Beans chart found below. Bring to a boil, reduce the heat to medium-low, and cover. Simmer gently until the beans are plump and tender to the bite. Never boil the beans furiously, as this will cause the skins to burst and result in a mushy bean. The beans are done when you can easily mash them with a fork. Also keep in mind that old beans may take longer to cook.

As a general rule, one cup of dried beans expands to three cups when cooked. To allow for this expansion, always use a large pot or kettle to cook them. It should not be more than three-quarters full of water.

Never add salt or acidic ingredients, such as tomatoes or lemon juice, to the pot until the beans are tender and nearly cooked. Acidic foods can cause the beans to harden and become tough, resulting in longer cooking time. Remember, cooking times vary according to the size, type, and age of the bean, as well as the presoaking method used.

When cooking at high altitudes, water boils at a lower temperature, causing the beans to cook more slowly. To hasten cooking time, add 1/4 teaspoon baking soda per cup of beans to the cooking water. This will help soften the outer skin of the beans. Pressure-cooking is another option.

Cooking Dried Beans

BEAN (1 CUP)	WATER	COOKING TIME	YIELD
Azuki	4 cups	1½ hours	2 cups
Black (turtle)	4 cups	1½ hours	2 cups
Cannellini	3 cups	2½ hours	2 cups
Chickpeas (garbanzo)	4 cups	3 hours	2 cups
Great Northern	3½ cups	2 hours	2 cups
Kidney	3 cups	2½ hours	2 cups
Lentils	3 cups	45 minutes	2¼ cups
Lima	2 cups	1½ hours	1¼ cups
Lima, baby	2 cups	1½ hours	1¾ cups
Navy	3 cups	2½ hours	2 cups
Pinto	3 cups	1½ cups	2 cups
Red	3 cups	3 hours	2 cups
Soybeans	4 cups	3+ hours	2 cups
Split peas	3 cups	45 minutes	2¼ cups

Egg and Dairy Alternatives

For those who avoid eggs or dairy products because of allergies or lactose intolerance, or through personal choice, a wide variety of nondairy milk and cheese alternatives are available. Most of the products in the following list are used in the recipes throughout this book, and are available in health food stores and most supermarkets. Look for high-quality brands such as Hain, Nasoya, Lisanatti, Soyco, and White Wave. (For additional information, see the Resource section.)

COCONUT MILK. Contrary to popular belief, coconut milk is not the liquid that is found in the center of coconuts. It is the thick flavorful "milk" which is extracted from grated coconut meat that has been steeped in hot water. Coconut milk can be substituted for dairy milk in most recipes in which coconut flavor is desired.

EGG ALTERNATIVES. In addition to commercial egg substitutes such as Egg Replacer by Ener-G Foods, there are a variety of other ingredient choices that serve as popular egg alternatives. The following commonly used ingredients are equivalent to one egg:

- ¼ cup tofu (any style) plus 1 teaspoon oil or water, blended in the food processor until smooth

- 1½ tablespoons flaxseeds mixed with ½ cup water

- 1 tablespoon Egg Replacer mixed with 2 tablespoons water

- 2 tablespoons soy flour mixed with 2 tablespoons water

- 2 tablespoons unbleached white flour

NAYONAISE. This tofu-based mayonnaise made by Nasoya contains no eggs and very little fat. For a soy mayonnaise you can prepare yourself, try the recipe on page 64.

NONDAIRY CHEESE. A number of cheeses made from soy and nut milks are now available in a variety of flavors, including Cheddar, Parmesan, and mozzarella. These products are available in reduced-fat versions as well. Look for brands such as Lisanatti and Soyco for quality products.

NUT MILKS. Creamy, mild-flavored nut milks are derived from most kinds of nuts (cashews and almonds are the most popular). The whole raw nuts are ground into powder, and then processed with water to form a creamy mixture. The resulting nut mixture is squeezed through a strainer to press out the milk and eliminate the pulp. Nut milks can be poured over cereal or used for cooking.

RICE MILK. Made from roasted grains of white or brown rice that have been pulverized to a powder and then cooked with water, mild-flavored rice milk comes in both plain and flavored varieties.

SOY MILK. Made from soybeans, this cholesterol-free milk has a light, nutty flavor and can be used in place of dairy milk in any recipe. It has about the same amount of protein, one-third the fat, and fifteen times as much iron as cow's milk. For the freshest soy milk varieties, look for those that come in aseptic containers. Soy milk also comes in dry varieties.

Meat and Poultry Alternatives

Protein-rich beans and legumes have long been popular alternatives to meats. In addition, with the rising interest in more vegetarian-style meals, a number of other plant-based options have gained popularity in recent years. Let's take a look at some of them, which are called for in a number of recipes throughout this book.

MEATLESS CRUMBLES. Ground meat-like crumbles made from soy or other vegetable proteins are becoming a popular meat alternative and are found in the freezer section of most grocery stores. They are used in dishes such as chili and tacos, which traditionally use ground meat.

POULTRY ALTERNATIVES. Typically made from textured soy protein, chicken-flavored cutlets and nuggets are now available in most health food stores and a number of major supermarkets. Brands like Harvest Direct offer these types of chicken alternatives, which can be marinated in a vegetarian chicken base or broth to achieve even greater chicken flavor. Eco-Cuisine offers a chicken quick mix powder made of soy, wheat gluten, and flavorings. After mixing this product with water, you can form it into "cutlets," and then cook according to the individual recipe. In addition to these commercial products, you can also use slices or chunks of tofu or tempeh, and flavor them in a vegetarian chicken-flavored marinade or broth. Tofu, especially, is neutral in taste and takes on the essence of its surrounding ingredients.

SEITAN. Made from the gluten found in whole wheat flour, seitan is a high-protein, low-fat food that is an excellent meat substitute. To make seitan, gluten dough is slowly simmered in a seasoned broth until it has a firm and chewy meat-like texture. It can be made at home from scratch or from a commercially available dry mix. Prepared seitan is also available in the refrigerated section of most health food stores. Recommended brands include White Wave, Up Country, and Harvest Direct.

Like tofu, seitan easily picks up the flavors of surrounding foods or liquids, and can be substituted for meat in just about any recipe. However, because it is precooked, seitan does not require the cooking time that meat does. When cooking seitan, do so only enough to warm it, or it will become dry and tough.

TEMPEH. Rich in protein and vitamin B_{12}, tempeh is a cultured soybean product that is native to Indonesia. During the tempeh-making process, partially cooked soybeans are incubated with a bacterium that acts as a binding agent. Easily digested, tempeh has a texture that is firm yet tender. It is highly perishable and must be used or frozen within a few days after it is made. Unlike tofu or seitan, tempeh must be cooked before it is eaten. Tempeh is found in the refrigerated or frozen foods sections of most natural foods stores.

TEXTURIZED VEGETABLE PROTEIN (TVP). A high-protein food made from defatted soy flour, TVP has the texture of ground meat. It comes packaged in dry crumbles or chunks that must be rehydrated with water.

TOFU. Long a staple in Asian diets, tofu is a high-protein, low-calorie, calcium-rich food that is convenient to use and easy to digest. It is a made from the extracted soy milk of cooked soybeans, and comes in regular and silken varieties. Tofu has a naturally bland taste that takes on the flavors of any food with which it is cooked.

Regular tofu comes in soft, firm, and extra-firm types, and must be refrigerated and used within a week. If regular tofu is being used in a cold dish, it should first be boiled for at least three minutes to kill any bacteria. *Silken tofu* is a very soft, custard-like tofu that comes in aseptic cardboard containers that do not need refrigeration until opened. The custardy texture of silken tofu, which also comes in soft, firm, and extra-firm types, makes it an excellent choice in many sauces and desserts.

TOFU CRUMBLES. Precooked tofu crumbles can be substituted for ground meat in most recipes. They come packaged and are found in health food and grocery stores alike.

VEGETARIAN LUNCHEON MEATS. Authentic-tasting bacon, ham, Canadian bacon, hot dogs, and pepperoni made from soy products are readily available in health food stores. Look for high-quality products made by Lightlife and Yves.

VEGETARIAN SAUSAGE. Low-fat soy-based Italian-style sausage, as well as Spanish-style chorizo sausage, are available in the refrigerator and/or frozen sections of most health food stores. Recommended brands include Lightlife and Yves.

Other Ingredients

A variety of other ingredients that are used in a number of recipes in this book are described in the following list.

ARROWROOT. This powered starch comes from the roots of the tropical arrowroot plant and makes an excellent thickening agent. It is also a good binder for meat and meatless loaves when eggs are not used. Before using, arrowroot powder should be dissolved in an equal amount of cold water (unless it is being used as a binder in a dry mix) and can replace cornstarch or kuzu in most recipes.

EGG ROLL WRAPPERS. Egg roll wrappers, which are typically used to house a variety of fillings, come in squares of different sizes. They can be purchased either in dried or ready-to-use form. You will find the ready-to-use type in the refrigerator section of most grocery stores. The dried variety must be softened in warm water for a few seconds before using.

FLAX MEAL. Made from ground flaxseeds, flax meal can be partially substituted for flour in cakes and breads, or mixed with water and used as an egg substitute in vegan dishes, especially baked goods. Once flaxseeds are ground, they tend to turn rancid quickly. If you have leftover meal, store it in an airtight container in the refrigerator.

FLAXSEEDS. Tiny oval-shaped flaxseeds are a rich source of beneficial omega-3 fatty acids. They can be sprinkled on cereal or added to breads and other baked goods for nutty flavor and added crunch.

KALAMATA OLIVES. This variety of Greek olives originated in the Greek city of Kalamata. Pickled in wine vinegar, Kalamata olives have a pronounced flavor and meaty texure.

RICE PAPER WRAPPERS. Made from rice flour, rice paper wrappers come in thin translucent sheets that are hard and brittle. Before using them as wrappers for fish, spring rolls, or other dishes, they must be softened in hot water for a few seconds. They are also called *spring roll wrappers.*

TIME TO GET STARTED

Now that you are armed and ready, it's time to roll up your sleeves and begin your culinary journey. Keep in mind that all of the recipes in this book have been kitchen-tested—sometimes more than once—to insure accurate ingredient amounts and cooking times. By following the recipes exactly as written, you will achieve successful results each time you make them. I suggest that once you have become familiar with preparing a recipe, you use it as a foundation to which you can add your own creative touches. Experiment. A recipe is always open to interpretation for the creative cook. Part of the excitement and joy of cooking is using your intuition to make the recipe sparkle. . . . So, let's get started.

2

Breakfast Fare

What's your breakfast pleasure at the start of the day? Is it a hearty meal of bacon and eggs? Or a fluffy stack of piping hot pancakes complete with fruit topping? Maybe you prefer a simple wedge of warm cornbread and a honey-sweetened cup of tea.

No matter what says "breakfast" to you, you will find it in this chapter. If it's eggs that you desire, you can choose dishes ranging from traditional and Spanish-style Eggs Benedict to satisfying omelets, flavorful frittatas, and savory quiches—all with vegan options. On those days that call for breakfast on the run, treat yourself to the Breakfast Sausage Wrap, made either with regular or with vegetarian-style sausage. It's a perfect choice. And on those leisurely weekend mornings, what could be more inviting than hot batter-dipped slices of Whole Wheat French Toast, or a stack of fluffy, golden brown Down Home Pancakes topped with syrup?

One thing is certain— these dishes, and all of the breakfast fare in this chapter, are real palate pleasers and a satisfying way to start the day.

Scrambled Eggs and Tofu with Spinach

Flavorful Canadian bacon gives this breakfast dish added spark.

1. Place the eggs and tofu in a blender, and blend until smooth.

2. Place the oil in a 10-inch frying pan, and heat over medium heat. Add the onion, bell pepper, Canadian bacon, and garlic. Sauté, stirring occasionally, for about 3 minutes, or until the onions are soft and almost transparent.

3. Pour the egg-tofu mixture over the vegetables, sprinkle with salt and pepper, and cook, stirring to scramble. Near the end of the cooking process, add the spinach, and continue cooking until done to taste.

4. Garnish with parsley, and serve hot.

MEATLESS CHOICE

- Instead of Canadian bacon, use vegetarian-style Canadian bacon, ham, or other breakfast meat alternative.

VEGAN CHOICE

- Replace the eggs with an additional 8 ounces of tofu, as well as ¼ cup soy mayonnaise (recipe on page 64), ½ teaspoon yellow prepared mustard, and ⅛ teaspoon turmeric. For a creamier dish, add extra mayonnaise.

Yield: 2 servings

4 eggs

1 cup (8 ounces) crumbled tofu

1 tablespoon canola or corn oil

½ cup finely diced onion

½ cup finely diced red bell pepper

¼ cup finely chopped Canadian bacon

1 teaspoon minced fresh garlic, or ½ teaspoon garlic powder

½ teaspoon sea salt

⅛ teaspoon ground black pepper

½ cup chopped fresh spinach, or ¼ cup frozen spinach, thawed and squeezed dry

2 tablespoons chopped fresh parsley

Crustless Canadian Bacon Quiche

*Sautéing the vegetables prevents this quiche
from becoming runny.*

Yield: 4 servings

2 tablespoons extra-virgin
olive oil

4 cups finely diced onions

1 cup grated carrots

1/2 cup finely chopped
Canadian bacon

1/2 teaspoon sea salt

1/8 teaspoon ground
black pepper

8 eggs

1/2 cup milk

1/4 cup grated Parmesan,
shredded Gruyère,
or crumbled aged goat cheese

1 1/2 cups coarse bread crumbs

1. Preheat the oven to 450°F.

2. Place the oil in a 10-inch ovenproof skillet, and heat over medium heat. Add the onions, carrots, Canadian bacon, salt, and pepper. Cover and cook, stirring occasionally, for 7 to 10 minutes, or until the onions are soft and translucent, but not brown.

3. Place the eggs and milk in a bowl, and beat together with a fork or wire whisk. Mix in the cheese and set aside.

4. Sprinkle the bread crumbs over the vegetables in the skillet, and then pour the egg mixture on top.

5. Place in the oven and bake for 5 minutes, or until the eggs are set and lightly browned.

6. Remove and cut into wedges. Serve hot or at room temperature.

MEATLESS CHOICE

- Instead of Canadian bacon, use vegetarian-style Canadian bacon, ham, or other breakfast meat alternative.

VEGAN CHOICE

- Replace the eggs with 2 cups Tofu Pâté (page 141), or a smooth blend of 2 cups (1 pound) crumbled tofu, 2 tablespoons arrowroot, 1 tablespoon sesame oil, and 1/4 teaspoon salt.
- Use soy milk instead of regular milk.
- Substitute soy Parmesan for regular Parmesan.

Traditional Frittata

The open-faced omelet known as a frittata is perfect when served for breakfast. It is also a good choice for a light lunch or dinner.

1. Place the eggs, milk, and salt in a bowl, and beat together with a fork or wire whisk.

2. Place the oil in a 7- or 8-inch omelet pan, and heat over medium-low heat. Add the egg mixture.

3. In another bowl, mix together the artichoke hearts, cheese, bell peppers, olives, and scallion, then sprinkle this mixture evenly over the egg. Cover and cook for about 5 minutes, or until the eggs are completely cooked. Be sure to keep the heat on medium-low to prevent the eggs on the bottom of the pan from burning. If you prefer, you can cook the frittata in a preheated 350°F oven for 5 to 8 minutes. Just be sure it is in an ovenproof pan.

4. Enjoy the frittata hot or at room temperature.

Yield: 1 serving

3 eggs

2 tablespoons milk

$\frac{1}{8}$ teaspoon sea salt

1 teaspoon canola oil

$\frac{1}{4}$ cup canned artichoke hearts

2 tablespoons finely diced Gouda cheese

2 tablespoons diced red bell peppers

2 tablespoons chopped Kalamata olives

1 tablespoon finely sliced scallion

VEGAN CHOICE

- Replace the eggs with $\frac{1}{2}$ cup Tofu Pâté (page 141), or a smooth blend of $\frac{1}{2}$ cup (4 ounces) crumbled tofu, 2 teaspoons arrowroot, and 1 teaspoon sesame oil. When adding this mixture to the hot pan, it must be spread onto the surface.

- Use soy milk instead of regular milk.

- Instead of the Gouda, use vegan-style mozzarella. You can also use 2 tablespoons crumbled tofu mixed with $\frac{1}{4}$ teaspoon nutritional yeast, which will give the mixture a cheesy flavor.

Breakfast Sausage Wrap

*I'm sure that today's popular sandwich wraps would have fared
well with the Earl of Sandwich. This wrap is a great way
to start the day—you can eat it on the run, or enjoy
it as part of a leisurely breakfast at home.*

Yield: 2 wraps

1 tablespoon extra-virgin
olive oil

1 small onion, peeled, halved,
and thinly sliced

¾ cup thinly sliced,
cooked breakfast sausage
or turkey sausage

1 cup cooked hash brown
potatoes

2 eggs

⅛ teaspoon sea salt

¼ cup sliced sundried tomatoes,
or roasted red bell peppers

2 flour tortillas
(10-inch rounds)

1. Place the oil in 10-inch frying pan, and heat over medium-low heat. Add the onions, and sauté, stirring occasionally, for 3 to 5 minutes, or until they are soft and almost transparent. Add the sausage and hash browns, and continue sautéing.

2. Beat the eggs until well blended and add them to the pan, along with the salt and sun-dried tomatoes. Continue to cook, stirring to scramble the eggs, until done to taste.

3. Lay out the tortillas on a flat surface, and place half of the filling mixture in the center of each. Fold the right and left sides of the tortilla over the filling, and then tightly roll up the tortilla into cylinder. Slice in the center at a 45-degree angle and serve.

MEATLESS CHOICE

- Instead of sausage, use vegetarian-style sausage or other breakfast meat alternative.

VEGAN CHOICE

- Replace the eggs with ¾ cup vegan version of Scrambled Eggs and Tofu with Spinach (page 25). Or use a blend of 1 cup (8 ounces) crumbled tofu, ¼ cup soy mayonnaise (recipe on page 64), ½ teaspoon yellow prepared mustard, and ⅛ teaspoon turmeric.

Eggs Benedict

Using reduced-fat Hollandaise sauce makes this dish a healthier choice than its traditional version. You can also try sautéed crabmeat or slices of fresh avocado, smoked salmon, or lobster tail instead of Canadian bacon.

1. Place the oil in 10-inch frying pan, and heat over medium-low heat. Add the Canadian bacon and cook 2 to 3 minutes on each side. Lightly toast the muffins.

2. Fill half of a 2-quart pot with water, add the vinegar, and bring to a boil over high heat. Reduce the heat to medium, and allow the water to simmer. Carefully crack each egg into the pot, and poach for 3 to 5 minutes to produce eggs with firm whites and soft yolks.

3. While the eggs are cooking, carefully add the asparagus spears to the same pot, and cook 2 to 3 minutes. Remove the asparagus, place on paper towels to drain, then cut each spear into thirds.

4. To serve, top each muffin half with 1 slice of Canadian bacon, 3 pieces of asparagus, 1 poached egg, and 1 tablespoon Hollandaise sauce. Sprinkle with salt and pepper.

Yield: 4 servings
(2 portions per serving)

1 tablespoon canola oil

8 thin slices Canadian bacon

4 whole wheat English muffins, or Grandma's Favorite Biscuits (page 35)

1 tablespoon cider vinegar

8 eggs

8 asparagus spears, tough stem ends removed

1 recipe Hollandaise Sauce (page 68)

Sea salt, to taste

Ground black pepper, to taste

MEATLESS CHOICE

• Instead of Canadian bacon, use vegetarian-style Canadian bacon or ham.

VEGAN CHOICE

• Replace the eggs with "poached" tofu. In a blender or food processor, prepare a mixture of 2 cups (1 pound) crumbled tofu, 1/2 cup soy mayonnaise (recipe on page 64), 2 tablespoons arrowroot, 1/2 teaspoon prepared mustard, and 1/8 teaspoon turmeric. Form the mixture into 8 equal scoops, and flatten each to a 1/2- to 3/4-inch thickness. Place the scoops on an oiled steamer rack set over boiling water. Cover and steam for about 7 minutes.

• Use plant-based Hollandaise Sauce (page 68)

Spanish Eggs Benedict

*Vegetable-based Spanish Sauce has very little fat and
no cholesterol; it provides a delicious twist to
this traditional breakfast dish.*

Yield: 4 servings
(2 portions per serving)

4 whole wheat English muffins,
or Grandma's Favorite Biscuits
(page 35)

I tablespoon cider vinegar

8 eggs

2 cups Spanish Sauce (page 88),
or your favorite fresh tomato sauce

2 tablespoons chopped
fresh parsley

1. Lightly toast the muffins.

2. Fill half of a 2-quart pot with water, add the vinegar, and bring to a boil over high heat. Reduce the heat to medium, and allow the water to simmer. Carefully crack each egg into the pot, and poach for 3 to 5 minutes to produce eggs with firm whites and soft yolks.

3. To serve, top each muffin half with ¼ cup Spanish Sauce and 1 poached egg. Garnish with parsley.

VEGAN CHOICE

- Replace the eggs with "poached" tofu. In a blender or food processor, prepare a mixture of 2 cups (1 pound) crumbled tofu, ¼ cup soy mayonnaise (recipe on page 64), 2 tablespoons arrowroot, ½ teaspoon prepared mustard, ⅛ teaspoon turmeric, and ¼ teaspoon salt. Form the mixture into 8 equal scoops, and flatten each to a ½- to ¾-inch thickness. Place the scoops on an oiled steamer rack set over boiling water. Cover and steam for about 7 minutes.

Whole Wheat French Toast

The low-cholesterol batter for this whole wheat version of French toast calls for egg whites instead of whole eggs.

1. Place the milk, water, and egg whites in a blender, and mix well. Add the brown sugar, vanilla extract, cinnamon, and salt, and blend until smooth. Pour the mixture into a shallow bowl, and set aside.

2. Place the butter on a griddle or in a large frying pan, and heat over medium heat (be careful not to burn).

3. Soak each slice of bread in the egg mixture for about 30 seconds, then remove and place in the heated pan.

4. Cook for 3 to 4 minutes, or until the bottom is brown. Using a spatula, turn the bread over and cook the other side for another 3 minutes.

5. Serve immediately drizzled with syrup.

Yield: 8 slices

3/4 cup milk

1/4 cup water

3 egg whites (from large eggs)

3 tablespoons brown sugar

1/2 teaspoon vanilla extract

1/8 teaspoon cinnamon

1/8 teaspoon sea salt

2 tablespoons butter

8 thick slices whole wheat bread

1/2 cup syrup of your choice

VEGAN CHOICE

- Replace the milk and water with 1¼ cups soy milk.
- Replace the egg whites with 3 tablespoons arrowroot or cornstarch, or 1½ tablespoons finely ground flax meal. (Any of these ingredients must be mixed with the soy milk.)
- Increase the vanilla to 1 teaspoon, the cinnamon to ¼ teaspoon, and the brown sugar to ¼ cup.
- Instead of butter, heat canola oil on the griddle.
- After soaking the bread, dip the bread into 1 cup unbleached white flour, coating both sides in the flour before cooking on the griddle. (Uncoated, the bread will stick to the griddle, no matter how much oil is on the griddle.)

Down Home Pancakes

*Try these pancakes with your favorite fruit topping.
I often serve them with plump ripe blueberries,
or freshly sliced peaches or apples.*

**Yield: 8 pancakes
(about 4 inches)**

I cup whole wheat flour

$\frac{1}{2}$ cup unbleached white flour

$\frac{1}{2}$ cup oat flour

2 teaspoons baking powder

I teaspoon cinnamon

$\frac{1}{2}$ teaspoon baking soda

$\frac{1}{4}$ teaspoon sea salt

I cup water

$\frac{3}{4}$ cup milk

I medium egg

I tablespoon maple syrup

I tablespoon softened butter

2 tablespoons canola oil

1. Combine the flours, baking powder, cinnamon, baking soda, and salt in a large mixing bowl. (If don't have oat flour on hand, you can make some by grinding $\frac{3}{4}$ cup of oatmeal in a blender on high speed for about 1 minute.) Set aside.

2. Place the water, milk, egg, maple syrup, and butter in another mixing bowl and blend together with a fork or wire whisk.

3. Pour the wet ingredients into the flour mixture, and mix together with a wooden spoon.

4. Heat the oil on a griddle or large frying pan over medium heat.

5. For each pancake, pour $\frac{1}{2}$ cup of batter onto the griddle, and spread into a 4-inch circle. Cook for about $1\frac{1}{2}$ minutes, or until the tops are bubbly and the edges are dry. Using a spatula, turn the pancakes over and cook for an additional minute, or until the bottoms are golden brown.

6. Serve hot with the topping of your choice.

VEGAN CHOICE

- Use soy milk instead of regular milk.
- In place of the egg, use a mixture of 1 tablespoon flax meal and $\frac{1}{4}$ cup water.
- Substitute canola oil for the butter.

Goat Cheese and Asparagus Omelet

Although goat cheese is my ingredient of choice in this recipe,
Gouda and mozzarella work equally well.

1. Place 1 teaspoon of the olive oil in an omelet pan, and heat over medium-low heat. Add the onions, bell peppers, asparagus, Canadian bacon, and basil, and sauté for 3 to 5 minutes, or until the onions are soft and almost transparent. Spoon the mixture into a dish and set aside.

2. Place the eggs, milk, and herbamare in a mixing bowl, and whip with a fork or wire whisk until frothy. Whipping the eggs properly is the key to a light omelet.

3. Add the remaining teaspoon of oil to the omelet pan, and heat up over medium-low heat. Add the egg mixture and cook, stirring gently until the eggs are almost set. To prevent burning, use medium-low heat when cooking.

4. Spoon the Canadian bacon-vegetable mixture over half the eggs, and top with cheese. Using a spatula, gently fold one-third of the omelet over the filling. Serve hot.

Yield: 1 serving

2 teaspoons extra-virgin olive oil

$\frac{1}{4}$ cup minced onion

$\frac{1}{4}$ cup diced red bell pepper

$\frac{1}{4}$ cup thinly sliced fresh asparagus, or frozen variety, thawed and squeezed dry

$\frac{1}{2}$ cup finely diced Canadian bacon

1 tablespoon shredded fresh basil

3 medium eggs

3 tablespoons milk

$\frac{1}{4}$ teaspoon herbamare, or $\frac{1}{8}$ teaspoon sea salt

1 ounce crumbled goat cheese

MEATLESS CHOICE

• Instead of Canadian bacon, use vegetarian-style Canadian bacon or ham.

VEGAN CHOICE

• Replace the eggs with a blend of 1 cup (8 ounces) crumbled tofu, 2 teaspoons soy mayonnaise (recipe on page 64), 2 teaspoons arrowroot, $\frac{1}{4}$ teaspoon yellow prepared mustard, and a pinch ($\frac{1}{16}$ teaspoon) turmeric.

• Mix all ingredients in a blender or food processor to form a smooth paste. Unlike regular eggs, this mixture must be spread onto the surface of the hot pan. Sauté for 3 to 5 minutes, then turn with a spatula. Continue with Step 4.

• Use vegan-style mozzarella instead of goat cheese.

Carrot Cornbread

Cornbread complements so many dishes in this book that I had to create a recipe for it. Enjoy this maple-sweetened version for breakfast or dessert. For a more savory cornbread, to accompany entrées such as Chili Mac (page 128) and Caribbean Black Beans (page 149), simply omit the maple syrup and vanilla extract.

Yield:
10-inch loaf

1 ¼ cups unbleached white flour

1 cup cornmeal

2 teaspoons baking powder

¼ teaspoon sea salt

1 egg

1 ¼ cups milk*

6 tablespoons maple syrup

¼ cup canola oil

½ teaspoon vanilla extract

¼ cup shredded carrots

1. Preheat the oven to 350°F. Oil and flour a 6-x-10-inch loaf pan.

2. In a large mixing bowl, combine the flour, cornmeal, baking powder, and salt.

3. In another mixing bowl, combine the egg, milk, maple syrup, oil, and vanilla, and mix well. Stir in the carrots. (To make carrot-coconut cornbread, replace the milk and oil with ¾ cup coconut milk.)

4. Add the cornmeal mixture to the liquid ingredients, and mix well with a wooden spoon.

5. Pour the batter into the prepared pan, and bake for 15 minutes, or just until a wooden toothpick inserted in the center of the loaf comes out clean.

6. Allow to sit for 10 minutes. Remove the loaf by inverting the pan onto a wire rack. Turn loaf right side up. Cool to room temperature, and serve.

VEGAN CHOICE

- In place of the egg, add 1 tablespoon flax meal to the dry ingredients and 2 tablespoons water to the wet ingredients.
- Use soy milk instead of regular milk.

Grandma's Favorite Biscuits

Father John Ostek, OFM, gave me this recipe,
which was handed down to him by his pioneer grandmother.

1. Preheat the oven to 425°F.

2. In a large mixing bowl, combine the flours, baking powder, salt, and butter. Mix well with a pastry blender, fork, or hands until the mixture resembles small peas.

3. Using a fork, stir in enough milk to hold the dough together (do this with as little mixing as possible). Form the dough into a ball.

4. Turn the dough onto a lightly floured surface. With floured hands, knead the dough about ten times before patting it evenly into a ½-inch thickness. Using a floured 2-inch biscuit cutter or the top of a glass tumbler, cut out circles of dough, and place them on an ungreased baking sheet. Combine the barley malt syrup and water, and brush on the tops of the dough.

5. Bake for about 12 to 15 minutes, or until the biscuits are light golden brown. Serve hot.

Yield: 18 biscuits

1¼ cups whole wheat pastry flour

1¼ cups unbleached white flour

1½ teaspoons baking powder

¾ teaspoon sea salt

5 tablespoons cold butter

⅞ cup milk

2 tablespoons barley malt or corn syrup (preferably dark)

2 tablespoons water

VEGAN CHOICE

- Replace the butter with corn oil or coconut butter.
- Use soy milk in place of regular milk.

3

Soup's On!

For me, there is probably nothing more warm and comforting than the heady aroma of homemade soup as it gently simmers on the stove. Simply wonderful.

This chapter offers a wide selection of soups ranging from the classic French Onion and traditional Scotch Broth to truly imaginative creations like Cream of Garlic Fennel Soup and Purée of Asparagus. For a light lunch or a prelude to a dinner, the Green Tomato Gazpacho and Mushroom Consommé are excellent choices. And when a heartier soup is what you desire, the Beef Soup Bourguignon is a clear winner, especially on cold winter evenings.

Because so many soups become even more delectable a day or two after they are made, I often prepare them in extra-large quantities—sometimes doubling or even tripling the recipe. That way, I can refrigerate a portion to enjoy the following day. Often, I freeze the leftovers to have on hand for "emergency" dinners, or to serve unexpected guests that happen to stop by. Bon Appetit!

Cream of Garlic Fennel Soup

Fennel adds a unique, flavorful twist to this creamy, heartwarming soup.

1. Place the oil and garlic in a 3-quart pot over medium-low heat. Sauté the garlic, stirring often, until it is golden brown. (Be careful not to burn it.) Remove most of the oil from the pot, and reserve it for future sautéing.

2. To the pot, along with the garlic, add the onions, fennel, and celery. Sauté for 7 to 10 minutes, or until the onions are soft and transparent.

3. Add the broth, potatoes, and salt, and simmer for about 20 minutes, or until all of the ingredients are very soft. Stir in the cream.

4. In batches, transfer the cooked ingredients to a blender, and process until smooth. Return to the pot and heat up.

5. Serve plain or topped with a splash of Basil Oil.

Yield: 8 servings

1 cup canola oil

2 cups fresh garlic cloves

2 cups coarsely chopped Spanish onions

1 ½ cups chopped fennel

1 cup finely diced celery

5 ½ cups chicken broth

2 cups peeled, shredded potatoes

1 ½ teaspoons sea salt

½ cup heavy cream

Basil Oil (page 68) for garnish, optional

MEATLESS CHOICE

• Instead of chicken broth, use vegetarian chicken broth or vegetable broth.

VEGAN CHOICE

• Use Cashew Cream (page 76) or other nondairy cream in place of regular heavy cream.

Purée of Asparagus Soup

*This velvety smooth soup has a delicate,
yet flavorful blend of ingredients.*

Yield: 3 servings

2 tablespoons canola oil

2 cups chopped fresh asparagus,
or frozen variety, thawed
and squeezed dry

1 cup chopped onions

¼ cup chopped carrots

¼ cup chopped celery

2 teaspoons minced fresh garlic

1 bay leaf

1½ teaspoons sea salt

½ teaspoon dry tarragon

4 cups water

1 cup frozen, thawed green peas

3 tablespoons sour cream
for garnish

1. In a 4-quart pot, add the oil, asparagus, onions, carrots, celery, garlic, bay leaf, salt, and tarragon, and place over medium heat. Sauté, stirring occasionally, for 10 minutes, or until the vegetables begin to soften.

2. Add the water, increase the heat to high, and bring to a boil. Reduce the heat to medium-low, and simmer covered for about 20 minutes, or until all of the ingredients are very soft.

3. In batches, transfer the ingredients to a blender, and process until smooth. Add the peas to the last batch being blended. Strain the soup through a sieve or strainer, transfer to the pot, and heat thoroughly.

4. Ladle the soup into bowls, top with a tablespoon of sour cream, and serve.

VEGAN CHOICE

- Replace the sour cream with a soy-based variety. Coconut Crème Frâiche (page 76) is another good option.

Green Tomato Gazpacho

*Although traditionally served chilled, this soup can also
be enjoyed hot, especially on cool autumn days.*

1. Heat the oil in a 4-quart pot over medium-low heat. Add the tomatoes, onions, potatoes, and garlic, and sauté, stirring occasionally, for about 5 minutes, or until the ingredients begin to soften.

2. Add the chicken broth to the pot, increase the heat to high, and bring to a boil. Reduce the heat to medium-low, and simmer covered for about 30 minutes. Stir in the cilantro, salt, and cumin.

3. In batches, transfer the cooked ingredients to a blender, and process until smooth.

4. Place the soup in a large bowl or container, cover, and refrigerate until chilled.

5. Serve plain or topped with a splash of Basil Oil.

Yield: 5 servings

2 tablespoons extra-virgin olive oil

4 cups chopped green tomatoes

1 cup chopped onions

1 cup peeled, diced potatoes

¾ cup garlic cloves

1 cup chicken broth

¼ cup chopped fresh cilantro, tightly packed

1 teaspoon sea salt

1 teaspoon ground cumin

Basil Oil (page 68) for garnish, optional

MEATLESS CHOICE

• Instead of chicken broth, use vegetarian chicken broth or vegetable broth.

Parsnip and Potato Purée

Thick, creamy, and delicious!

1. Place the potatoes and parsnips in a 4-quart pot, add enough water to cover, and place over medium-high heat. Cook about 30 minutes, or until the vegetables are soft. Drain.

2. Transfer the potatoes and parsnips to an electric mixing bowl, along with the remaining ingredients. Mix on slow speed for about 1 minute. Increase the speed to medium-high and continue mixing the ingredients for about 4 minutes, or until the mixture has the consistency of heavy cream.

3. Transfer the soup to the pot, and heat thoroughly.

4. Ladle the hot soup into bowls and serve.

VEGAN CHOICE

- Use soy milk instead of regular milk.

Cream of Mushroom Soup

For an interesting flavor option,
try adding ¼ cup Pernod to this soup.

1. Place the oil, mushrooms, onions, potatoes, and garlic in a 4-quart pot, and place over medium-low heat. Sauté, stirring occasionally, for about 10 minutes, or until the vegetables begin to soften.

2. Add the chicken broth, cream, bay leaf, and salt to the pot, and bring to a boil over high heat. Reduce the heat to medium-low, and simmer covered for about 20 minutes.

3. Remove and discard the bay leaf. In batches, transfer the cooked ingredients to a blender, and process until smooth.

4. Return the soup to the pan and heat thoroughly.

5. Enjoy as is, or drizzled with a little Basil or Chive Oil.

MEATLESS CHOICE

- Instead of chicken broth, use vegetable broth or a mixture of 2 tablespoons vegetarian chicken broth powder and 4 cups water.

VEGAN CHOICE

- Replace the heavy cream with soy or cashew cream.

Yield: 4 servings

2 tablespoons canola oil

4 cups chopped button mushrooms

2 cups coarsely chopped onions

1 cup unpeeled, shredded red potatoes

1 tablespoon minced fresh garlic

4 cups chicken broth

½ cup heavy cream

1 bay leaf

¼ teaspoon salt

Basil Oil (page 68) for garnish, optional

French Onion Soup

It's a classic!

1. Preheat the oven broiler to 425°F.

2. In a large stockpot over medium heat, melt the butter, then add the onions, carrots, garlic, salt, and pepper. Sauté, stirring occasionally, for 10 to 15 minutes, or until the onions are soft and transparent.

3. Add the chicken broth and wine to the pot, and continue cooking for another 15 minutes.

4. Divide the soup among six deep soup bowls or crocks. Place a slice of bread on top of each bowl, then top with 1/4 cup of cheese.

5. Place the bowls under the broiler for about 1 minute, or until the cheese is melted.

6. Serve piping hot.

MEATLESS CHOICE

- Instead of chicken broth, use vegetable broth or a mixture of 2 tablespoons vegetarian chicken broth powder and 4 cups water.

VEGAN CHOICE

- Use canola or sesame oil instead of butter.
- Substitute shredded soy mozzarella for the Gouda or Gruyère.

Scotch Broth

*You can use an inexpensive cut of lamb
in this Scottish favorite.*

1. Heat the oil in a 4-quart pot over medium heat, and add the lamb, onions, carrots, celery, rutabaga, leeks, thyme, and barley. Sauté, stirring occasionally, for about 15 minutes, or until the lamb is cooked and the onions are transparent.

2. Add the broth, increase the heat to high, and bring to a boil. Reduce the heat to medium-low, cover, and simmer about 30 minutes, or until the barley is fully cooked.

3. Dissolve the miso in a little broth, then add it to the pot along with the salt and pepper.

4. Simmer the soup another 5 minutes before serving.

MEATLESS CHOICE

- Replace the lamb with ground seitan, rehydrated TVP (texturized vegetable protein), or another meat alternative.

- Instead of lamb broth, use water or vegetable broth.

Yield: 6 servings

2 tablespoons canola or sesame oil

1/4 pound trimmed, finely diced lamb

2/3 cup diced onions

1/2 cup diced carrots

1/4 cup diced celery

1 cup diced rutabaga

1 cup thinly sliced leeks,
or 3 to 4 scallions

1/2 teaspoon thyme

6 tablespoons pearl barley

7 1/2 cups lamb broth

1/2 teaspoon sea salt

1/4 teaspoon white pepper

2 tablespoons barley miso
or beef base

Beef Soup Bourguignon

This hearty soup makes a great meal when accompanied by a crisp green salad and some fresh bread.

Yield: 4 servings

1 tablespoon sesame oil

1 cup thinly sliced beef (flank steak or any inexpensive cut will work)

1 1/2 cups diced onion

1/4 cup sliced celery

3/4 cup sliced mushrooms

2 teaspoon minced fresh garlic

1 1/2 teaspoons chopped fresh basil

1/3 teaspoon ground black pepper

1 1/2 cups water

1/2 cup dry red wine

3/4 cup tomato purée

1 tablespoon beef base

Sea salt, to taste

Chopped fresh parsley for garnish

1. Heat the oil in a 4-quart pot over medium heat. Add the beef, onions, celery, mushrooms, garlic, basil, and pepper. Sauté, stirring occasionally, for 10 to 15 minutes, or until the beef is cooked and the onions are transparent.

2. Add the water, wine, tomato purée, beef base, and salt. Cover and cook for 20 to 30 minutes over medium-low heat to allow the flavors to develop.

3. Ladle the hot soup into bowls, garnish with parsley, and serve.

MEATLESS CHOICE

- Replace the beef with sliced seitan. As seitan is already cooked, add it to the soup along with the other ingredients in Step 2.

- Use dark barley miso instead of beef base.

Mushroom Consommé

A consommé is a rich clarified meat, vegetable, or fish broth that can be enjoyed as a soup or used as a base for sauce. A double consommé is one that has been cooked down to half its volume, making it very rich. For a sea vegetable consommé, replace the mushrooms in the following recipe with ½ cup wakame.

1. Combine all of the ingredients in a 4-quart pot, place over medium-high heat, and bring to a boil. Reduce the heat to low, cover, and simmer for 1 to 2 hours. (The longer the broth simmers, the richer it will become.)

2. Remove the mushrooms from the pot and thinly slice.

3. Ladle the consommé into bowls, garnish with the sliced mushrooms, and serve piping hot.

MEATLESS CHOICE

- Replace the beef base with 2 tablespoons vegetable base or vegetarian beef base. You can also use ¼ cup tamari soy sauce.

Yield: 5 servings

1 cup thinly sliced onions

½ cup thinly sliced carrots

½ cup thinly sliced celery

¾ cup dry mushrooms, such as morels or King Bolete

6 cups water

2 tablespoons beef base

1 teaspoon minced fresh garlic

Potato-Cucumber Vichyssoise

Vichyssoise is a rich, creamy potato-leek soup that is traditionally served cold with a garnish of chopped chives. This modern interpretation has a chicken broth base, and calls for cucumbers and herbs instead of leeks. It is a "natural" choice when you have leftover potatoes on hand.

1. Place the potatoes and enough water to cover in a 2-quart pot over high heat. Just as the water begins to boil, reduce the heat to low and simmer for about 15 minutes, or until the potatoes are soft. Drain.

2. Transfer the potatoes and all of the remaining ingredients to a blender, and blend until smooth.

3. Place the soup in a large bowl or container, cover, and refrigerate until chilled.

4. Ladle the soup into bowls, garnish with chives, and serve.

MEATLESS CHOICE

- Instead of chicken broth, use vegetarian chicken broth or vegetable broth.

Yield: 6 servings

2 cups peeled, diced potatoes (preferably Yukon gold)

4 cups peeled, seeded, and coarsely chopped cucumbers

2 cups chicken broth

1 heaping tablespoon fresh tarragon

1 teaspoon dried dill

3/4 teaspoon sea salt, or to taste

1/8 teaspoon ground black pepper

Chopped chives for garnish

4

The Salad Bowl

Once upon a time, a salad was nothing more than an uninspiring bowl of torn iceberg lettuce, a slice or two of tomato, and a splash of bland bottled dressing. (Yawn.) Today's salad has emerged from its former place in the shadows to become a highly anticipated prelude to an entrée, or even a main course. And why not? The salad has evolved into a spectacular showcase of flavors, textures, and vibrant colors.

Exotic greens and vegetables, once considered specialty items, are now readily available in most supermarkets. And the sky's the limit when it comes to the ingredients you can add to make your salad creation complete (and just the way you like it). Imagine a bed of your favorite greens topped with a colorful mélange of roasted vegetables, marinated tuna, or spicy grilled chicken strips. In addition, cooked grains and pasta, plump legumes, and oven-roasted nuts can all offer wonderful textures to your salad masterpiece, while crumbled cheese or slices of fruit can add a spark of flavor.

If you're in the mood for a spectacular main dish salad, or a simple accompaniment, you'll find a wealth of recipes from which to choose on the pages that follow.

Mediterranean Pasta Salad

The Sauce Niçoise and feta cheese are the defining flavors in this hearty salad.

1. In a large mixing bowl, add the pasta, green and red bell peppers, olive oil, salt, black pepper, feta cheese, and Sauce Niçoise. Mix well. (This pasta mixture will keep in the refrigerator for a week.)

2. On individual salad plates, place 2 cups of the salad greens. Then top with 1 cup of the pasta mixture. Serve immediately.

VEGAN CHOICE

- Replace the feta cheese with soy Parmesan.
- Use the vegan Sauce Niçoise option (page 82).

Yield: 4 servings

4 cups cooked rigatoni pasta

$\frac{1}{4}$ cup diced green bell pepper

$\frac{1}{4}$ cup diced red bell pepper

2 tablespoons extra-virgin olive oil

$\frac{1}{4}$ teaspoon sea salt

$\frac{1}{4}$ teaspoon ground black pepper

$\frac{1}{4}$ cup crumbled feta cheese

1 cup Sauce Niçoise (page 82)

8 cups salad greens of choice

Red Cabbage Slaw

This salad is as eye-appealing as it is flavorful.
It is best to let this salad sit for a day before serving it.

Yield: 6 servings

6 cups shredded red cabbage

¼ cup apple cider vinegar

½ teaspoon sea salt

2 cups chopped Granny
Smith apples

2 tablespoons sugar

1 cup roasted whole pecans
(see inset below for
roasting instructions)

1½ cups Apricot-Raspberry
Vinaigrette (page 63)

1. In a deep 10-inch skillet, add the cabbage, vinegar, and salt, and place over medium heat. Sauté, stirring occasionally, for 5 minutes, or until the cabbage just starts to wilt.

2. Transfer the cabbage to a large mixing bowl, along with the apples, sugar, pecans, and Apricot-Raspberry Vinaigrette. Toss the ingredients well.

3. Cover the bowl and refrigerate until chilled before serving.

ROASTING NUTS

Nuts are a great source of protein and a popular substitute for meat in a wide variety of dishes. I like to keep roasted nuts on hand to add to a dish at a moment's notice. Stored properly, nuts can stay fresh for a long time. Follow these steps for dry-roasting most nut varieties.

1. Spread nuts out in a single layer on a baking sheet, and place in a preheated 275°F oven.

2. Roast the nuts, stirring them occasionally, until they begin to brown and give off a pleasant aroma. Roasting times will vary depending on the oven temperature, as well as the size and thickness of the nut. A small pine nut will cook more quickly than a walnut, and thinly sliced almonds will brown much more quickly than the whole variety. Cooking times generally range from 3 to 25 minutes.

3. Keep an eye on nuts as they roast. Set a timer or stay near the oven. As soon as you begin to smell them roasting, they are almost done. It usually takes less than a minute from the moment a nut begins to burn to the point of its being ruined.

4. Remove the roasted nuts from the oven and immediately transfer them to another tray to cool. If you leave them on the hot roasting tray, they will continue to cook—and possibly burn.

5. After the nuts have cooled, place them in an airtight container. Store them in the refrigerator or freezer, where they will keep for 2 to 3 months.

Cottage Cheese Salad

*Sautéed onions and dill help turn plain cottage cheese
into something special.*

1. Place the oil, onions, dill, and salt in a small sauté pan over medium heat. Sauté, stirring occasionally, for 5 to 7 minutes, or until the onions are soft and transparent. Remove from the heat and let cool.

2. In a medium-sized mixing bowl, combine the cottage cheese and chives. Add the cooled onion mixture and mix well.

3. Enjoy as is, or atop a bed of leafy greens.

Yield: 4 servings

1½ teaspoons canola or
extra-virgin olive oil

½ cup peeled, diced onions

¼ teaspoon dry dill weed

¼ teaspoon sea salt

2 cups cottage cheese

2 tablespoons chopped chives

VEGAN CHOICE

• Replace the cottage cheese with 1 cup crumbled tofu blended with ½ cup soy mayonnaise. (For soy mayonnaise recipe, see page 64.)

Oriental Pasta Salad

Despite its long ingredient list,
this colorful salad is easy to make.

Yield: 8 servings

2 cups spiral-shaped pasta

¼ teaspoon sea salt

¼ cup sweet white miso

¼ cup rice vinegar

2 tablespoons sesame oil

1 tablespoon minced fresh garlic

½ teaspoon ground ginger

2 cups shredded carrots

2 cups sliced red onions

1½ cups sliced bok choy
(preferably baby)

1 cup diced red bell pepper

12 cups chopped romaine
lettuce

4 boiled eggs, peeled
and chopped

1. Cook the pasta al dente according to package directions. Drain the pasta and run it under cold water to cool.

2. In a mixing bowl, combine the salt, miso, rice vinegar, sesame oil, garlic, and ginger. Mix well.

3. In a large salad bowl, combine the pasta, carrots, onions, bok choy, and bell pepper. Add the vinegar-miso mixture and toss well. Refrigerate at least one hour.

4. To serve, place 1½ cups of lettuce on individual salad plates, top with 1 cup of pasta, and sprinkle chopped egg on top.

VEGAN CHOICE

- Instead of the eggs, use 8 ounces crumbled or finely diced extra-firm tofu that has been tossed with 1 tablespoon tamari or other soy sauce, and lightly browned in a skillet along with 1 tablespoon sesame oil.

Three-Grain Salad

*I love the texture of the different grains
in this flavorful salad, which I serve warm.*

1. In a bowl filled with cold water, add the barley and rice. Swish the grains with your hand to wash them. Drain.

2. Bring the water to a boil in a 2-quart pot over medium heat. Add the grains and a pinch of salt. Cover and simmer about 40 minutes, or until the grains are soft. Set aside.

3. Heat the oil in a 10-inch skillet over medium heat. Add the leeks, carrots, and corn, and sauté for about 3 minutes. Transfer to a mixing bowl.

4. Add the cooked grains to the bowl, along with the ginger, salt, and dressing. Mix well. Enjoy as is.

Yield: 2 servings

½ cup pearl barley

½ cup brown basmati rice

½ cup wild rice

3½ cups water

1 teaspoon extra-virgin olive oil

1½ cups thinly sliced leeks

½ cup julienne carrots

½ cup whole kernel corn

1 tablespoon minced pickled ginger

¼ teaspoon sea salt

¾ cup Ginger-Miso Dressing (page 60)

Roasted Vegetable Salad with Grilled Chicken

This salad can be served cold on a bed of salad greens, or warm along with some brown rice.

1. Preheat the oven to 400°F.

2. In a large mixing bowl, toss together the carrots, onions, Jerusalem artichokes, salt, and 2 tablespoons of the oil. Spread the vegetables in a single layer on a baking sheet, and roast for about 20 minutes.

3. Toss the Brussels sprouts with the remaining teaspoon of oil, and add them to the roasting vegetables. Continue to roast for another 10 minutes.

4. Remove the vegetables from the oven, and transfer them to a mixing bowl. Add the Sauce Niçoise, and mix well.

5. Serve immediately, topped with grilled chicken.

MEATLESS CHOICE

- Replace the chicken with a vegetarian chicken alternative, such as Chiken Brest by Harvest Direct.

VEGAN CHOICE

- Replace the Sauce Niçoise with the vegan option (page 82).

Yield: 6 servings

2 cups carrots, cut into thin circles

2 cups coarsely diced onions

2 cups Jerusalem artichoke roots, cut into thin circles

¼ teaspoon sea salt

2 tablespoons plus 1 teaspoon canola oil

2 cups halved Brussels sprouts

1 cup Sauce Niçoise (page 82)

12 ounces grilled chicken, cut into strips

Tuna Salad Niçoise

The traditional Niçoise Salad calls for tuna.
I recommend fresh tuna, but canned tuna works just as well.
I often enjoy this salad as a summer entrée
that is served over greens.

Yield: 6 servings

1 ½ pounds fresh tuna

3 tablespoons canola oil

¼–½ teaspoon sea salt

4 cups Sauce Niçoise
(page 82)

9 cups chopped salad greens
of choice

1. Preheat the oven broiler. Lightly oil a baking sheet and set aside.

2. Cut the tuna into ½-inch-thick slices, and place on the baking sheet. Brush with oil, sprinkle with salt, and broil for 5 to 7 minutes, or until the fish is opaque and easily flakes with a fork.

3. Once the tuna is cool, cut it into bite-size pieces and place in a mixing bowl. Add the sauce and toss to coat well.

4. Place 1½ cups of salad greens on individual plates. Top with equal portions of tuna, and serve.

VEGAN CHOICE

- Replace the tuna with Sea Vegetable Tofu (page 137).
- Replace the Sauce Niçoise with the vegan option (page 82).

Black-Eyed Peas and Corn Salad

This salad makes a great summer lunch or dinner salad. And black-eyed peas cook quicker than most traditional bean varieties.

1. Bring the water to boil in a 3-quart pot. Add the black-eyed peas, and reduce the heat to medium. Add the carrots and onions, and cook for 40 to 50 minutes, or until the carrots and peas are tender.

2. Add the corn and sun-dried tomatoes during the last 10 minutes of cooking. Drain the mixture, and transfer it to a mixing bowl. Cool for about 15 minutes.

3. Add the cilantro, oil, vinegar, salt, and mustard to the bowl, and mix well.

4. Divide the salad greens among individual salad plates, and top with the black-eyed pea and corn mixture. Serve cold or at room temperature.

Yield: 5 servings

4 cups water

I cup dried black-eyed peas

I cup diced carrots

I ½ cups diced onions

I cup cooked whole kernel corn

½ cup sun-dried tomatoes, or I cup diced fresh tomatoes

¼ cup chopped fresh cilantro

¼ cup extra-virgin olive oil

¼ cup balsamic vinegar

I ½ teaspoons sea salt

2 tablespoons Dijon mustard

8 cups salad greens of choice

Tuna Salad Niçoise

The traditional Niçoise Salad calls for tuna.
I recommend fresh tuna, but canned tuna works just as well.
I often enjoy this salad as a summer entrée
that is served over greens.

Yield: 6 servings

1 ½ pounds fresh tuna

3 tablespoons canola oil

¼–½ teaspoon sea salt

4 cups Sauce Niçoise
(page 82)

9 cups chopped salad greens
of choice

1. Preheat the oven broiler. Lightly oil a baking sheet and set aside.

2. Cut the tuna into ½-inch-thick slices, and place on the baking sheet. Brush with oil, sprinkle with salt, and broil for 5 to 7 minutes, or until the fish is opaque and easily flakes with a fork.

3. Once the tuna is cool, cut it into bite-size pieces and place in a mixing bowl. Add the sauce and toss to coat well.

4. Place 1½ cups of salad greens on individual plates. Top with equal portions of tuna, and serve.

VEGAN CHOICE

- Replace the tuna with Sea Vegetable Tofu (page 137).
- Replace the Sauce Niçoise with the vegan option (page 82).

Black-Eyed Peas
and Corn Salad

This salad makes a great summer lunch or dinner salad. And black-eyed peas cook quicker than most traditional bean varieties.

Yield: 5 servings

4 cups water

1 cup dried black-eyed peas

1 cup diced carrots

1 ½ cups diced onions

1 cup cooked whole kernel corn

½ cup sun-dried tomatoes,
or 1 cup diced fresh tomatoes

¼ cup chopped fresh cilantro

¼ cup extra-virgin olive oil

¼ cup balsamic vinegar

1 ½ teaspoons sea salt

2 tablespoons Dijon mustard

8 cups salad greens of choice

1. Bring the water to boil in a 3-quart pot. Add the black-eyed peas, and reduce the heat to medium. Add the carrots and onions, and cook for 40 to 50 minutes, or until the carrots and peas are tender.

2. Add the corn and sun-dried tomatoes during the last 10 minutes of cooking. Drain the mixture, and transfer it to a mixing bowl. Cool for about 15 minutes.

3. Add the cilantro, oil, vinegar, salt, and mustard to the bowl, and mix well.

4. Divide the salad greens among individual salad plates, and top with the black-eyed pea and corn mixture. Serve cold or at room temperature.

Egg Salad

*Enjoy this flavorful egg salad on a bed of lettuce
or as a sandwich filling.*

1. Bring a 2-quart pot of water to a simmer over medium heat. Carefully add the eggs to the pot, and cook for 10 to 12 minutes. Place the cooked eggs in a bowl of cold water to cool them and to prevent them from turning green.

2. Peel and finely chop the eggs, and place them in a mixing bowl with the remaining ingredients.

3. Enjoy immediately, or store in a covered container and refrigerate until ready to use.

VEGAN CHOICE

- Replace the eggs with 1 cup crumbled tofu.
- Instead of regular mayonnaise, use soy mayonnaise. (For soy mayonnaise recipe, see page 64.)

Yield: 3 servings

4 eggs

½ cup finely diced onion

½ cup finely diced celery

½ cup mayonnaise

1 teaspoon canola oil

1 teaspoon prepared yellow mustard

¼ teaspoon sea salt

⅛ teaspoon ground black pepper

Tofu "Egg" Salad

This "eggless" egg salad has always been a favorite
among my vegetarian friends and family members.

Yield: 4 servings

1 tablespoons canola oil

¼ cup finely diced onions

¼ cup finely diced celery

¾ cup crushed tofu

½ cup Soy Mayonnaise (page 64)

¼ teaspoon garlic powder

¼ teaspoon sea salt

⅛ teaspoon ground black pepper

⅛ teaspoon turmeric

1. Heat the oil in a 2-quart pot over medium heat. Add the onions and celery, and sauté, stirring occasionally, for 7 to 10 minutes, or until the onions are soft and transparent. Transfer the mixture to a bowl and allow to cool about 10 minutes.

2. To the cooled onion mixture, add the tofu, mayonnaise, garlic powder, salt, pepper, and turmeric. Mix well.

3. Enjoy immediately, or store in a covered container and refrigerate until ready to use.

Ginger-Miso Dressing

This dressing has wonderful texture, taste, and color.
The potatoes serve as a fat replacement, the mirin neutralizes
any acidity, and the oil brings out the flavors of miso and ginger.

Yield: About 2½ cups

¾ cup mashed potatoes

½ cup canola oil

½ cup water

¼ cup white miso

¼ cup mirin

¼ cup cider vinegar

1 tablespoon sugar

¾ teaspoon ground ginger

1. Place all of the ingredients in a blender, and blend until smooth.

2. Use immediately, or place in a covered container and refrigerate.

Cucumber Sour Cream Dressing

This cool, creamy dressing is especially good drizzled over garden vegetable salads. You can also use it to replace the mayonnaise in pasta salads. For a citrus-flavored version, replace the vinegar with lime juice and the zest of one fresh lime.

1. Place all of the ingredients except the cucumber in a blender, and blend until smooth.

2. Add the cucumbers and stir to mix well.

3. Use immediately, or place in a covered container and refrigerate.

VEGAN CHOICE

- Replace the sour cream with soy-based sour cream, or cashew sour cream.
- Instead of honey, use ¼ cup corn syrup.

Yield:
About 4 cups

12 ounces sour cream

1 ¼ cups water

1 ¼ cups extra-virgin olive oil

1 small onion, peeled

½ cup apple cider vinegar

16 sprigs fresh parsley

2 tablespoons honey

1 ½ teaspoons sea salt

1 ¼ teaspoons dry dill weed

1 ¼ teaspoons prepared yellow mustard

1 ½ cups peeled, seeded, minced cucumbers

Sesame-Mustard Vinaigrette

This tangy dressing is great on any fresh green salad,
as well as on pasta and roasted vegetable salads.
It is also a wonderful addition to grilled meats.

Yield: About 3 cups

¼ cup sesame seeds

1 cup Dijon mustard

1 cup canola oil

½ cup mirin

½ cup cider vinegar

2 tablespoons sugar

2 teaspoons mustard powder

½ teaspoon sea salt

1. Place the sesame seeds in a dry 10-inch skillet, and roast over medium heat. Stir the seeds frequently for 3 to 5 minutes, or until the seeds are browned. (Be careful not to burn them.) Immediately transfer the seeds to a blender and pulverize.

2. Add the remaining ingredients to the blender, and blend until smooth.

3. Use immediately, or place in a covered container and refrigerate.

Orange Vinaigrette

A splash of this mild dressing will add a light,
refreshing citrus flavor to your favorite green salad.
You can also enjoy it as a dip for raw or fried vegetables.

Yield: About 1 cup

½ cup orange juice

¼ cup canola oil

¼ cup rice vinegar

2 tablespoons sweet white miso

1. Place all of the ingredients in a blender, and blend until smooth.

2. Use immediately, or place in a covered container and refrigerate.

Down Home Pancakes (page 32)
[TOP LEFT]
Breakfast Sausage Wrap (page 28)
[TOP RIGHT]
Spanish Eggs Benedict (page 30)
[BOTTOM]

Potato-Cucumber Vichyssoise (page 48)
[TOP LEFT]

Beef Soup Bourguignon (page 46)
[TOP RIGHT]

Goat Cheese and Asparagus Omelet (page 33)
[BOTTOM]

Cranberry Port Vinaigrette

*This dressing, which is one of my favorites,
won a gold medal in the 1996 International Culinary Olympics.
I always serve it with Pâté Français (page 138).*

1. Place all of the ingredients in a blender, and blend until smooth.

2. Use immediately, or place in a covered container and refrigerate.

Yield: About 1½ cups

1/4 cup cranberry juice concentrate

1/4 cup balsamic vinegar

1/4 cup port wine

1/4 cup water

1/4 cup olive oil

1½ tablespoons chopped fresh basil

1 tablespoon honey

2 teaspoons Dijon mustard

1 teaspoon minced fresh garlic

1/4 teaspoon sea salt

Apricot-Raspberry Vinaigrette

*This dressing complements most leafy green salads,
especially those with nuts or fruits.*

1. Place all of the ingredients in a blender, and blend until smooth.

2. Use immediately, or place in a covered container and refrigerate.

Yield: About 1½ cups

4 fresh or canned apricots, pitted and halved

1/4 cup raspberry jam

1/4 cup apple cider vinegar

1/4 cup olive oil

1/4 teaspoon sea salt

Modern Mayonnaise

*Traditionally, eggs and oil are the main ingredients needed
to make mayonnaise. This modern version uses tofu to
replace some of the oil called for in the original recipe.
A blender makes it a snap to combine the ingredients.
For a vegan version, see the Soy Mayonnaise below.*

Yield: About 1½ cups

6 ounces silken tofu

½ cup vegetable oil

1 egg

1 tablespoon lemon juice

1 teaspoon prepared
yellow mustard

½ teaspoon sea salt

1. Place all of the ingredients in a blender, and blend until smooth.

2. Use immediately, or place in a covered container and refrigerate.

Soy Mayonnaise

Here's a quick and easy-to-make vegan mayonnaise.

Yield: About 1½ cups

12.3-ounce package extra-firm
silken tofu

¼ cup canola oil

1 tablespoon lemon juice

1 teaspoon prepared
yellow mustard

½ teaspoon sea salt

1. Place all of the ingredients in a blender, and blend until smooth.

2. Use immediately, or place in a covered container and refrigerate.

5

Sensational Sauces and Condiments

The right sauce or condiment can elevate a favorite dish to a spectacular sit-up-and-take-notice affair, providing a subtle finishing touch or an electrifying burst of flavor. And don't believe that great sauces will take hours to prepare. And as you'll see, the majority of recipes found in this chapter can be ready in less than thirty minutes, and they can often be stored for weeks, allowing you to enjoy your creation in a wide range of fabulous dishes.

And talk about choices! The following pages offer an incredible number of sauces and condiments to accompany all types of dishes. You'll find rich cream sauces, flavorful pestos, savory brown sauces, and exciting salsas, ranging in flavor from mild and mellow to hot and spicy. There are bread spreads and herb-flavored oils, as well as tasty condiments like caramelized onions and preserved lemons.

So whether you are looking for a creamy spread for your favorite sandwich or a gourmet sauce to turn a ho-hum dish into company fare, this chapter has just what you're looking for—and just the way you like it.

Roasted Rosemary Potato Butter

I first tried potato butter in a Greek restaurant in Chicago, and fell in love with it. Try it on bread or as a sandwich spread.

1. Preheat the oven to 400°F.

2. In a mixing bowl, toss together the potatoes, oil, and salt. Transfer to a small roasting pan, and place in the oven uncovered. Cook for about 5 minutes, then add the garlic. Continue to cook about 15 minutes, or until the potatoes are soft when pierced with a fork.

3. Transfer the cooked potatoes to a food processor along with the water, rosemary, and parsley. Process until smooth.

4. Place the mixture in a covered container, and store in the refrigerator, where it will keep for about two weeks.

5. Use as you would butter.

Yield: About 2 cups

2½ cups finely diced potatoes

¼ cup extra-virgin olive oil

¼ teaspoon sea salt

⅓ cup minced fresh garlic tossed with 2 tablespoons extra-virgin olive oil, or ½ cup Garlic Confit (page 75)

¼ cup water

⅛ teaspoon dry rosemary

2 tablespoons chopped fresh parsley

Basil Oil

By their very nature, oils are flavor enhancers.
Infusing an oil with a fresh herb or spice will further fortify its
flavor. The oil in this recipe is infused with sweet, aromatic basil.

Yield:
About 6 tablespoons

¼ cup extra-virgin olive oil

¼ cup chopped basil, or
2 tablespoons Basil Paste
(page 69)

1. In a small sauté pan, add 1 tablespoon olive oil and the basil. Place over low heat, and sauté for about 2 minutes, or until the basil turns a rich green. Immediately remove the pan from the heat and add the remaining oil.

2. Allow the oil to sit for a minute, then transfer it to a covered container. (You can store the oil as is, or strain it to remove the solids.)

3. Refrigerated, the oil will last up to three months. In the freezer, it will keep for six months.

Hollandaise Sauce

This is a simple interpretation of a classical sauce.
If using on seafood, add a teaspoon of dried dill.

Yield: About 1¼ cups

6 ounces extra-firm silken tofu

¼ pound unsalted butter, melted

I egg yolk

2 teaspoons lemon juice

¼ teaspoon sea salt

1. Place ingredients in a blender, and blend until smooth.

2. Transfer mixture to a 1-quart saucepan and place over low heat. Slowly stir the mixture until it is almost boiling.

3. Use immediately, or transfer to a covered container and store in the refrigerator. It will keep for about one week.

VEGAN CHOICE

• In place of the butter, use soy butter or margarine.
• Use 2 teaspoons flax meal mixed with 3 tablespoons water as a substitute for the egg yolk.

Basil Paste

When frozen, you can shave this paste on a plate of hot pasta,
giving it the appearance of shaved chocolate.

1. Place the potatoes and enough water to cover in a 1-quart saucepan over medium heat. Simmer 10 to 15 minutes, or until the potatoes are completely cooked and the water is almost evaporated. Drain the remaining water.

2. Transfer the potatoes to the blender, along with the oil, lemon juice, salt, and half of the basil. Blend at low speed, while carefully pressing the basil to the bottom with a spatula.

3. When the basil is pulverized, add the cashew butter and the remaining basil. Blend on medium speed until a smooth paste forms.

4. Transfer the paste to a covered container and store in the refrigerator, where it will last up to two weeks. To freeze, put the paste in an ice cube tray. Once frozen, remove the pesto "cubes," transfer them to an airtight container, and return to the freezer.
Use as needed.

Yield:
About 2 cups

1/4 cup peeled, shredded potatoes

1/4 cup extra-virgin olive oil

1/4 cup lemon juice

1/2 teaspoon sea salt

8 cups loosely packed fresh basil

2 tablespoons raw cashew butter, or 3 tablespoons pine nuts

Red Pepper Pesto

This recipe has excellent color, texture, and flavor.
Toss it with a bowl of pasta or try it as a topping for burgers.

1. Oven-roast the bell pepper according to the inset instructions on page 71.

2. Place all of the ingredients in a blender, and blend until smooth.

3. Transfer the mixture to a covered container and store in the refrigerator, where it will last up to two weeks. To freeze, put the mixture in an ice cube tray. Once frozen, remove the pesto "cubes," transfer them to an airtight container, and return to the freezer. Use as needed.

VEGAN CHOICE

• Use soy Parmesan in place of the regular variety.

Yield: About 1¾ cups

2 large red bell peppers

¼ cup roasted pistachios
(see inset on page 52
for roasting instructions)

3 tablespoons minced fresh garlic
tossed with 1 tablespoon
extra-virgin olive oil,
or ¼ cup Garlic Confit (page 75)

¼ cup extra-virgin olive oil

2 tablespoons grated
Parmesan cheese

2 tablespoons chopped
fresh cilantro

½ teaspoon sea salt

Walnut Pesto

In addition to tossing this walnut pesto with pasta,
try it as a sandwich spread for an interesting change.

1. Place all of the ingredients in a blender, and blend until smooth.

2. Transfer the mixture to a covered container and store in the refrigerator, where it will last up to two weeks. To freeze, put the mixture in an ice cube tray. Once frozen, remove the pesto "cubes," transfer them to an airtight container, and return to the freezer. Use as needed.

VEGAN CHOICE

• Use soy Parmesan in place of the regular variety.

Yield: About 1½ cups

½ cup roasted walnuts
(see inset on page 52
for roasting instructions)

1 cup chopped fresh basil

⅓ cup minced fresh garlic

¼ cup Parmesan cheese

¼ cup plus 2 tablespoons
extra-virgin olive oil

¼ teaspoon sea salt

ROASTING BELL PEPPERS

Fresh roasted bell peppers have an incomparable flavor and velvety texture. And the good news is that they are easy to prepare. You can roast peppers on a barbecue grill, in the oven, or under a broiler. Just follow the simple instructions below:

1. Halve and seed the peppers, then brush their skins with a little olive oil.

2. If using a broiler or grill, place the peppers about 4 to 5 inches from the heat source. Cook, turning once or twice, for 5 to 7 minutes, or until they are soft and the skin is blackened and blistered. If roasting in the oven, place the pepper halves on a baking sheet and cook at 325°F for about 30 to 40 minutes, or until the peppers are soft.

3. Transfer the roasted peppers to a brown paper bag or sealed plastic container, and let them steam for about 10 minutes to loosen the skin. When they are cool enough to handle, remove and discard their skin.

4. Serve the peppers, or place them in a tightly sealed container and store in the refrigerator, where they will keep for about one week. You can also freeze roasted peppers for up to six months.

Coconut au Gratin Topping

Au gratin is a French term referring to a dish that is topped with bread crumbs and usually butter and/or grated cheese, and then browned in an oven. This version uses coconut instead of cheese.

Yield: About 2 cups

1/3 cup softened butter

1 tablespoon minced fresh garlic

1 cup unsweetened flaked coconut

1/2 cup sherry wine

1/2 cup whole wheat bread crumbs

3 tablespoons minced fresh parsley

3/4 teaspoon sea salt

1/4 teaspoon ground paprika

1. Place the butter in a sauté pan and place over medium heat. Add the garlic and coconut, and sauté for about 2 minutes, or until the garlic begins to soften and brown (be careful not to burn).

2. Add the sherry and continue to cook for about 10 minutes, or until the wine has evaporated.

3. Add the remaining ingredients to the pan, mix well, and remove from the heat.

4. Place the mixture in a sealed container and store in the refrigerator, where it will last up to three months. Frozen, it will keep for about six months.

VEGAN CHOICE

• Use 1/3 cup peanut oil in place of the butter.

Caramelized Onions

*Browned caramelized onions add the perfect touch
of sweetness to many bland foods.*

Yield:
About 2½ cups

3 large Spanish onions, halved
lengthwise then cut into
⅛-inch slices

¼ teaspoon sea salt

2 tablespoons canola oil

3 tablespoons water

1. Place a deep 10- to 12-inch skillet over medium heat.
Add the onions and salt, and dry sauté, stirring occasionally, for about 10 minutes, or until the onions caramelize to
a rich golden brown.

2. Add the oil and water to the skillet, and mix with the
onions. Stir to deglaze the pan (remove the bits of onion
that have stuck to it). Transfer the onions to a bowl and cool.

3. Enjoy hot, warm, or at room temperature. To store, place the cooled
onions in a covered container and refrigerate or freeze. Refrigerated, they
will last about two weeks; frozen, they will keep for about six months.

Soy Cashew Sour Cream

*This sour cream has a rich, creamy texture, with a slight hint
of lemon. Use it as you would regular sour cream.*

Yield: About 1 cup

1 tablespoon raw cashews

6 ounces silken tofu

¼ cup canola oil

2 tablespoons lemon juice

¼ teaspoon sea salt

1. Place the cashews in a blender, and blend into a fine
meal.

2. Add the remaining ingredients, and blend until the
mixture is smooth and creamy.

3. Transfer the mixture to a covered container, and store
in the refrigerator or freezer. Refrigerated, it will last about
one month; frozen, it will keep for about six months. (After thawing the
frozen sour cream, you will have to reblend it before using.)

Red Onions with Merlot Confit

This recipe is especially good with any sausage dish, although it adds a delicious spark of flavor to tofu dishes and vegetable sides. Try it with the Hazelnut-Crusted Stuffed Portabellas (page 148).

Yield:
About 2 cups

1 tablespoon sesame oil

4 cups thickly sliced red onion rings

1 tablespoon minced fresh garlic

1 teaspoon dry thyme

1/4 teaspoon sea salt

3/4 cup Merlot wine

1 tablespoon sugar

1. In a 10-inch sauté pan, heat the oil over medium heat. Add the onions, garlic, thyme, and salt, and sauté, stirring occasionally, for 5 minutes, or until the onions are soft and translucent.

2. Stir in the wine and sugar, and continue to cook for 10 to 15 minutes, or until the liquid is reduced to about 1/4 cup.

3. Enjoy hot, warm, or at room temperature. To store, place the cooled onions in a covered container and refrigerate or freeze. Refrigerated, they will last about two weeks; frozen, they will keep for about six months.

CONFIT

Confit (pronounced kon•FEE) hails from the Gascony region of France. It is typically a preserved meat, usually a fatty variety such as duck or pork. The meat is salted and cooked slowly, then packed in a crock or pot and covered with its cooking fat, which acts as a seal. The preserved meat becomes buttery tender as it ages.

Confit is not limited to meat. Onions, garlic, and lemons are popular confit choices. After cooking out their moisture, the foods are preserved in oil. Try the Red Onions with Merlot Confit (above) and the Garlic Confit (page 75). They are wonderful accompaniments to a wide variety of dishes.

Garlic Confit

Because this confit stores so well, you can make it in large quantities to always have on hand.

Yield: About 3 cups

4 cups peeled fresh
garlic cloves

2 to 2½ cups canola oil

1. Place the garlic in a 2-quart saucepan, and add enough oil to cover the cloves. Set over low heat, and slow-cook for 1½ hours, or until the cloves no longer emit bubbles. (The bubbles are a sign that moisture is escaping from the garlic.)

2. Be sure to keep the heat low to prevent the cloves from browning.

3. Place the cooked garlic along with the oil in a covered container, and store in the refrigerator, where it will keep for up to three months.

Preserved Lemons

Enjoy these lemon slices as an accompaniment to most fresh vegetable side dishes, or add them to your favorite green salad. I always serve them with Moroccan Ratatouille (page 162).

Yield: About 2 cups

4 medium-sized lemons

4 cups plus 2 cups water

¼ cup sugar

1 tablespoon sea salt

1. Cut the lemons into ¼-inch slices (2 cups).

2. Place the slices and 4 cups of water in a 2-quart saucepan, and place over medium heat. Simmer for 30 minutes. Drain the lemon slices, and discard the liquid.

3. Return the lemon slices to the pan along with the sugar, salt, and the remaining 2 cups of water. Simmer over medium heat for 20 to 30 minutes, or until the water is nearly evaporated. Remove from the heat and let cool.

4. Transfer the lemons to a covered container, and store in the refrigerator or freezer. Refrigerated, they will last about two weeks; frozen, they will keep for about six months.

Coconut Crème Frâiche

Traditionally made in France as a cultured cream product, crème frâiche can also be made by adding vinegar to heavy cream. Either way, the result is a tart, tangy product with the same rich flavor as sour cream. The following is a modern nondairy version that goes well with Caribbean Black Beans (page 149).

Yield:
About ¾ cup

½ cup coconut milk

¼ cup powdered milk

2 teaspoons rice vinegar

1. Place all of the ingredients in a blender, and blend until smooth.

2. Transfer the mixture to a covered container, and store in the refrigerator or freezer. Refrigerated, it will last about two months; frozen, it will keep for about six months. (After thawing the frozen crème frâiche, you will have to reblend it before using.)

VEGAN CHOICE

• Substitute soy or coconut milk powder for the regular milk powder.

Cashew Cream

Similar to traditional whipping cream, cashew cream serves as a great base for many sauces.

Yield:
About 1½ cups

1 cup raw cashew pieces

1 cup water

1. Place the cashews and water in a blender and blend for 3 minutes, or until the mixture is smooth.

2. Transfer to a covered container and store in the refrigerator or freezer. Refrigerated, it will last for about one week; frozen, it will keep up to six months.

Harissa Sauce

Harissa is a hot and spicy North African condiment made from oil, chilies, garlic, cumin, coriander, and caraway seeds. There are many versions of this sauce, depending on the country of origin. It is typically served with couscous, soups, and dried meat.

Yield: About 5 cups

1 tablespoon ground cumin

1 tablespoon ground coriander

1 teaspoon ground cloves

1 teaspoon ground cardamom

1/4 cup extra-virgin olive oil

3 cups chopped carrots

2 cups diced onions

2 cups chopped red bell peppers

3/4 cup peeled fresh garlic cloves

1 teaspoon ground ginger

1 teaspoon sea salt

1 cup water

1. In a small mixing bowl, combine the cumin, coriander, cloves, and cardamom. Mix well and set aside.

2. Heat the oil in a 2-quart saucepan over medium heat. Add the carrots, onions, bell peppers, garlic, ginger, and salt. Sauté the mixture for 15 minutes, or until the vegetables are cooked. Add the water, cover, and continue to cook for another 10 minutes. Remove the pan from the heat and set aside.

3. In a blender, add the sautéed vegetables along with 1 tablespoon of the spice blend (for a spicy sauce, add 2 tablespoons). Gently pulse the mixture 3 to 5 times, then blend on low speed until the mixture is smooth.

4. Use immediately, or transfer to a covered container and store in the refrigerator, where it will keep for about two weeks. In the freezer, it will last about six months.

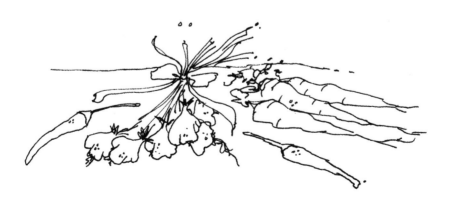

Avocado-Cucumber Salsa

Not only is this salsa great as a dip for chips, it is also a wonderful dressing for a simple green salad.

Yield: About 1½ cups

1 ripe avocado, peeled, pitted, and finely diced

1 medium-sized cucumber, peeled, seeded, and diced

½ cup sour cream

2 tablespoons lime or lemon juice

2 tablespoons chopped fresh cilantro

½ teaspoon minced fresh garlic

½ teaspoon sea salt

1. Place all of the ingredients in a medium-sized mixing bowl and combine well.

2. Cover and refrigerate for at least 30 minutes before serving. Stored in a covered container, this salsa will last for about one week in the refrigerator.

VEGAN CHOICE

• Instead of regular sour cream, use a soy-based variety, such as Soy Cashew Sour Cream (page 73). Or you can use a soy-based mayonnaise, such as Soy Mayonnaise (page 64). If using mayonnaise, reduce the salt to ¼ teaspoon.

Lemon Olive Blanc

The blended flavors of olive oil and lemon make this sauce an excellent choice to serve over fresh vegetable dishes as well as seafood.

Yield: About 1 cup

¾ cup cooked white navy beans

½ cup extra-virgin olive oil

3 tablespoons lemon juice

¼ teaspoon salt

1. Place all ingredients in a blender and process until smooth and creamy.

2. Warm in a saucepan before using. To store, place the sauce in a covered container and refrigerate for up to three weeks.

Lemon Beurre Blanc

Try this creamy sauce warm on seafood and vegetables, as well as on grilled chicken and pasta dishes. The navy beans, which are used instead of oil, act as an excellent emulsifier, while keeping the fat content of the sauce low.

Yield: About ¾ cup

½ cup (4 ounces) unsalted butter, melted

½ cup cooked white navy beans

2 tablespoons lemon juice

¼ teaspoon salt

1. Place all ingredients in a blender and process until smooth and creamy.

2. Warm in a saucepan before using. Store in a covered container and refrigerate for up to three weeks.

Onion-Garlic Cream Sauce

Smooth, flavorful, and easy to prepare!

 Yield: About 2¼ cups

½ cup canola oil

2 cups diced Spanish onions

1 cup peeled fresh garlic cloves

½ cup cream

½ teaspoon sea salt

1. Heat the oil in a 2-quart saucepan over medium-low heat. Add the onions and garlic, and sauté, covered, for about 30 minutes, or until they are soft and beginning to brown.

2. Reserving the oil for another use, drain the cooked onion and garlic, and transfer to a blender along with the cream and salt. Blend until smooth.

3. Use immediately, or transfer to a covered container, and store in the refrigerator or freezer. Refrigerated, the sauce will last about one week.

VEGAN CHOICE

• Use soy milk in place of the cream.

French Brown Sauce

This flavorful sauce is perfect with most meats and poultry dishes.
It is also great on top of cooked grains.

Yield: About 3 cups

2 tablespoons canola or sesame oil

1 cup coarsely diced onions

1 cup shredded
or finely diced carrots

1 cup finely diced celery

1 tablespoon tamari or other
soy sauce, or 1 teaspoon
caramel coloring*

5 teaspoons beef bouillon

1 tablespoon minced fresh garlic

2 tablespoons chopped fresh basil,
or 2 teaspoons dried

2 teaspoons dry thyme

1/2 cup unbleached white flour

4 1/4 cups water

1/2 cup red wine

1/2 cup tomato paste

1. Heat the oil in a 2-quart saucepan over medium heat. Add the onions, carrots, celery, soy sauce, bouillon, garlic, basil, and thyme, and sauté, stirring occasionally, for 15 minutes, or until the vegetables are beginning to soften and brown.

2. Mix in the flour and stir to combine. Continue to cook for 5 minutes, then stir in half of the water. Add the wine, tomato paste, and remaining water, and stir well. Cover and simmer for 15 minutes.

3. Strain the sauce before using. Serve immediately, or transfer to a covered container and store in the refrigerator, where it will keep for four to six weeks. You can also freeze the sauce for up to six months.

* Instead of soy sauce, you can use 2 tablespoons of gills from the underside of Portabella mushroom caps. This will add dark color and earthy flavor to the sauce.

MEATLESS CHOICE

• Replace the beef bouillon with vegetarian beef bouillon.

Bigarade Sauce

If you have leftover French Brown Sauce on hand, try turning it into this savory sweet-and-sour creation. Traditionally served with duck, Bigarade Sauce works just as well with chicken and seitan.

1. Place the jelly in a 1-quart saucepan and warm over medium heat. Add the remaining ingredients, and mix well.

2. Bring to a simmer, and cook for 5 minutes. Serve immediately, or transfer to a covered container. Refrigerate for up to two weeks, or freeze for up to six months.

Yield: About 2 cups

¼ cup currant jelly

1 ½ cups French Brown Sauce (page 80)

¼ cup Balsamic Demi-Glace (page 83)

1 tablespoon orange zest

¼ cup red wine

VEGAN CHOICE

• Replace beef bouillon in the French Brown Sauce with vegetarian beef bouillon.

Béchamel Sauce

Béchamel is another sauce that is a French classic. My version is a little thicker than the traditional. If you prefer a thinner variety, add more milk or cream (soy or dairy).

1. Combine the milk, salt, and nutmeg in a 1-quart saucepan, and place over medium heat.

2. Add roux and stir with wire whisk until sauce thickens.

3. Use immediately, or transfer to a covered container and store in the refrigerator, where it will keep for about two weeks.

Yield: About 2 cups

2¼ cups whole milk

⅛ teaspoon sea salt

1/16 teaspoon ground nutmeg

¼ cup Roux (page 86), or mixture of ¼ cup unbleached white flour plus 2 tablespoons canola oil

VEGAN CHOICE

• Instead of milk, use soy milk or a blend of 2 cups soy milk and ¼ cup Cashew Cream (page 76).

Sauce Niçoise

*When a food is prepared à la Niçoise, it means "as it
is prepared in the French city of Nice." Characteristically,
the dish contains tomatoes, black olives, garlic, and anchovies.
Salade Niçoise, which also includes green beans, onions, tuna,
and hard-boiled eggs, is probably the most famous of this style dish.
You will find that Sauce Niçoise, which calls for green olives instead
of the usual black variety, is a great choice to flavor pasta salads,
vegetables, and grain dishes, as well as seafood and poultry.*

Yield:
About 6 cups

2 tablespoons extra-virgin
olive oil

1 ½ cups finely diced
Spanish onions

3 tablespoons chopped garlic

1 cup chopped pimento-stuffed
green olives

3 cups chopped canned tomatoes

¾ cup whole capers

¼ cup lemon juice

½ teaspoon black pepper

¼ cup water

1 tablespoon chopped anchovies

1. Heat the oil in a 2-quart saucepan over medium-low heat. Add the onions and garlic, and sauté for about 10 minutes, or until the onions are beginning to soften.

2. Add the olives, tomatoes, capers, lemon juice, pepper, water, and anchovies to the pan, and simmer for about 20 minutes, stirring occasionally.

3. Use immediately, or store in a covered container in the refrigerator, where it will last for months. It is best to let the sauce sit for at least a day to allow its flavors to develop.

VEGAN CHOICE

• Eliminate the anchovies.

Balsamic Demi-Glace

My idea for this sauce came while cooking with Peter Poole and his lovely wife, Nancy. It was served with a nut-crusted tofu. The sauce keeps for months with refrigeration and is one that you will always want on hand. It goes particularly well with chicken, tofu, and seitan.

1. In a 1-quart saucepan on medium heat, add the brown sugar and stir continually for about 5 minutes, or until lightly caramelized.

2. Add ¾ cup of the water, and the vinegar, wine, and tamari, and bring to a simmer. The caramelized sugar will harden, but don't let it stick to the bottom of the pan, or it will burn.

3. Cover and simmer for 5 to 10 minutes, stirring occasionally, until the caramelized sugar dissolves. Remove from the heat.

4. In a small mixing bowl, combine the cornstarch with 2 tablespoons water, and mix well. Stir into the sugar mixture.

5. Return the pot to medium heat, stirring constantly until the sauce thickens.

6. Allow the sauce to cool before transferring it to a covered container and refrigerating until ready to use. It will last for months in the refrigerator.

Yield:
About 1¾ cups

¾ cup brown sugar

¾ cup plus 2 tablespoons water

½ cup balsamic vinegar

6 tablespoons red wine

3 tablespoons tamari soy sauce

2 tablespoons cornstarch or arrowroot powder

Italian Tomato Sauce

This simple tomato sauce is characteristic of the
ones popular in Northern Italy.

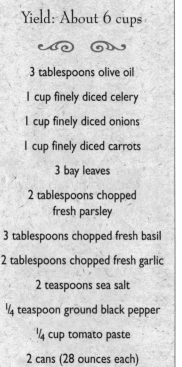

Yield: About 6 cups

3 tablespoons olive oil

1 cup finely diced celery

1 cup finely diced onions

1 cup finely diced carrots

3 bay leaves

2 tablespoons chopped
fresh parsley

3 tablespoons chopped fresh basil

2 tablespoons chopped fresh garlic

2 teaspoons sea salt

1/4 teaspoon ground black pepper

1/4 cup tomato paste

2 cans (28 ounces each)
crushed tomatoes

1. Place all of the ingredients, except the tomato paste and crushed tomatoes, in a 3- or 4-quart saucepan, and set over medium heat. Sauté for about 5 minutes, or until the onion is soft and translucent. Be careful not to burn the garlic.

2. Add the tomato paste and crushed tomatoes, and stir until well combined with the sautéing vegetables. Increase the heat to high, bring the ingredients to a boil, then reduce the heat to very low. Simmer, stirring often to prevent the sauce from burning, for 60 to 90 minutes. The longer the sauce simmers, the thicker it will get.

3. Use immediately, or allow the sauce to cool before transferring it to a covered container, and storing it in the refrigerator or freezer. Refrigerated, the sauce will keep for about three weeks. In the freezer, it will last about six months.

Asian Peanut Sauce

*This sauce, which is a great accompaniment to grilled foods,
is also a wonderful addition to pasta.*

1. Combine all of the ingredients in a 1-quart saucepan, and place over medium heat. Heat until the sauce is just warm.

2. Use immediately, or transfer to a covered container and store in the refrigerator, where it will keep for about one week.

Yield: About ¾ cup

¼ cup creamy peanut butter

¼ cup coconut milk

¼ cup water

2 tablespoons lemon juice

½ teaspoon sea salt

½ teaspoon garlic powder

½ teaspoon Five-Spice powder

Roasted Bell Pepper Sauce

*You can use any color bell pepper you prefer
for this incomparable sauce.*

1. Oven-roast the bell pepper according to the inset instructions on page 71.

2. Place all of the ingredients in a blender, and blend until smooth.

3. Transfer the mixture to a 1-quart saucepan and place over low heat. Stir the mixture and bring it to a boil.

4. Serve immediately, or place in a covered container and store in the refrigerator, where it will keep for about three weeks.

Yield: About 1½ cups

1 large yellow bell pepper,
or colored pepper of choice

6 ounces extra-firm
silken tofu

¼ cup white wine

¼ cup extra-virgin olive oil

2 tablespoons lemon juice

½ teaspoon sea salt

Moo Goo Gai Pan Sauce

This traditionally vegetarian sauce is superb with stir-fries.
If you will be using it with a chicken stir-fry,
add 1 teaspoon chicken base to the sauce.

Yield: About 2 cups

¼ cup sesame oil

4½ teaspoons minced
fresh ginger

4½ teaspoons minced
fresh garlic

2 cups water

¼ cup sherry wine

1½ teaspoons sea salt

⅛ teaspoon white pepper

3 tablespoons arrowroot

1. Heat the oil in a 1-quart saucepan over medium heat. Add the ginger and garlic, and sauté for about 3 minutes, or until they are soft, but not browned.

2. Add the water, wine, salt, and pepper, and stir well. Bring to a simmer, then turn off the heat.

3. Stir in the arrowroot, turn the heat to medium, and continue to stir for 3 to 5 minutes, or until the sauce is thick.

4. Use immediately, or transfer to a covered container and store in the refrigerator, where it will keep for about one week.

Roux

A mixture of flour and fat—usually butter—roux is used as a
thickener for sauces, soups, and stews. The recipe below
calls for vegetable oil instead of butter, and it yields
one cup—enough to thicken a half gallon of liquid.
I always have roux on hand to use as needed.

Yield: About 1 cup

1 cup unbleached white flour

½ cup canola oil

1. In a mixing bowl, combine the flour and oil, and mix well.

2. Place the mixture in a covered container and store in the refrigerator.

Oriental Pasta Salad (page 54)
[TOP LEFT]
Hazelnut-Crusted Stuffed Portabellas (page 148)
[RIGHT]
Red Cabbage Slaw (page 52)
[BOTTOM LEFT]

Salmon Niçoise (page 108)
[TOP RIGHT]

Halibut Spring Rolls (page 113)
with Risotto Pesto (page 163)
[LEFT]

Sea Vegetable Corn Cakes (page 152)
with Red Pepper Pesto (page 70),
and Preserved Lemons (page 75)
[BOTTOM RIGHT]

Velouté Sauce

This white sauce is the basis for many classical French sauces. It is also one of my favorites. For a really rich, thick version, add ½ cup heavy cream to the ingredients below. For a vegan version, use Cashew Cream (page 76) instead of heavy cream.

1. Melt the butter in a 3-quart saucepan over medium heat. Add the onions, celery, carrot, and garlic. Sauté for 5 minutes, or until the onion is transparent.

2. Add the thyme, bay leaf, parsley, black pepper, chicken base, and water. Mix well, reduce the heat to medium-low, and simmer for 1 hour.

3. Strain the mixture and return it to the pan. Add the roux and salt, and stir with a wire whisk until the sauce thickens.

4. Use immediately, or transfer to a covered container and store in the refrigerator, where it will keep for about two weeks.

VEGAN CHOICE

- Replace the butter with sesame or canola oil.
- Use vegetarian chicken base instead of regular chicken base.

Yield: About 3 cups

1 tablespoon butter

1 cup diced onions

1 cup diced celery

1 cup diced carrots

2 teaspoons minced fresh garlic

¼ teaspoon dried thyme

1 bay leaf

3 sprigs parsley, chopped

⅛ teaspoon black pepper

1 tablespoon chicken base

2 quarts water

½ cup Roux (page 86), or mixture of ½ cup unbleached white flour plus ¼ cup canola oil

¼ teaspoon sea salt

Spanish Sauce

Traditional Spanish sauce is very thick and often used as a flavorful omelet filling. This version, which is thinner than the original, goes very well with Eggs Benedict (page 29) and Shrimp Creole (page 112).

Yield: About 6 cups

1 tablespoon extra-virgin olive oil

1 cup thinly sliced onions

1/2 cup grated or
very thinly sliced celery

1/2 cup sliced button mushrooms

1 tablespoon minced
fresh garlic

1/2 teaspoon dry thyme

1 bay leaf

3 cups tomato purée

1 cup diced tomatoes

1 cup water

1/4 cup sliced green olives

3/4 teaspoon sea salt

1 cup diced green bell peppers

1. Heat the oil in a 2-quart saucepan over medium heat. Add the onions, celery, mushrooms, garlic, thyme, and bay leaf. Sauté the mixture for 5 minutes, or until the onions are soft and transparent.

2. Add the tomato purée, diced tomatoes, water, olives, and salt, and bring to a simmer.

3. Add the bell peppers, and cook another 2 minutes.

4. Serve immediately, or transfer to a covered container and store in the refrigerator, where it will keep for about two weeks.

Ron's Gremolada

An aromatic blend of chopped parsley, garlic, and lemon zest,
Gremolada is used traditionally as a garnish for rice and other
grains. It is also gaining popularity as an excellent salt substitute.
My version, which is great on seafood, meat, and spicy
vegetarian entrées, is presented below.

1. Place all of the ingredients in a mixing bowl, and toss together just before serving. (If prepared too far in advance, the parsley will wilt.)

2. Sprinkle on food before serving.

Yield: About 1 cup

2 tablespoons chopped
roasted garlic
(roasting instructions below)

2 tablespoons Orange Vinaigrette
(page 62),
or a blend of 2 teaspoons
orange juice concentrate,
2 teaspoons olive oil, and
2 teaspoons cider or
balsamic vinegar

2 tablespoons lemon zest

$\frac{1}{2}$ cup coarsely chopped
fresh parsley

$\frac{1}{4}$ cup coarsely shredded
red radishes

2 teaspoons extra-virgin olive oil

ROASTING GARLIC

Nothing is more tantalizing than the aromatic smell of roasting garlic as it wafts its way through the house. When slow-roasted, garlic cloves are transformed into honey-colored morsels that literally melt in your mouth. The soft, caramelized cloves can be added to a variety of dishes or used as a spread on bread or crackers.

Although terra cotta garlic roasters are available, you can easily oven-roast garlic without them. Simply follow the instructions below.

1. Remove the papery outer skin from a head of garlic, but do not peel or separate the cloves.

2. Place the garlic in a small baking dish, and drizzle with 1 or 2 teaspoons of olive oil. Cover tightly with foil, and bake in a 350°F oven for about 30 to 40 minutes, or until the cloves are soft.

3. Remove the garlic cloves by slipping them out of their skins, and either spreading the garlic on bread or using it in a recipe.

Forager's Sauce

This fresh-tasting sauce will keep for months in the refrigerator,
and is very good with either poultry or seitan.

Yield: About 3 cups

¼ cup canola oil

I cup finely chopped
Portabella mushrooms

½ cup finely diced
Spanish onions

½ cup finely diced
red bell pepper

I tablespoon minced
fresh garlic

½ teaspoon chopped
dry rosemary

½ teaspoon chopped dry basil

I cup finely diced tomatoes

I cup red wine

¼ cup tamari soy sauce

1. Heat the oil in a 2-quart saucepan over medium heat. Add the mushrooms, onions, bell pepper, garlic, rosemary, and basil, and sauté for about 10 minutes, or until the vegetables begin to soften.

2. Add the tomatoes, wine, and tamari to the pan, and simmer for about 20 minutes. Remove from the heat.

3. Use immediately, or allow the sauce to cool, then store in a covered container in the refrigerator. It will keep for a few months.

6

Super Sandwiches and Fresh Breads

Is your idea of a sandwich one of those those brown-bagged white-bread specials that your mom used to make? Forget about it! Believe it or not, the sandwich is among the most popular items offered by many of the best-known restaurants and bistros in the country. Chefs have stretched their imaginations to the limit to create taste-tempting sandwiches that offer both satisfaction and visual appeal. And this chapter presents recipes that rival any you might find on a restaurant menu.

You'll find twists on traditional sandwich fare, as well as new recipes that combine unusual yet truly delicious ingredient choices. Are you a fan of grilled cheese? What about egg salad? If you are, be sure to try my Grilled Cheese and Egg Salad Sandwich, complete with vegan alternatives. If you love the smoky flavor of grilled vegetables, the Cuban-style Pressed Grilled Vegetable Sandwich is an excellent choice. And if you're looking for a really hearty dish, the As-You-Like-It Hoagie is a sure winner.

So forget those boring sandwiches of the past, and get ready to enjoy gourmet fare that even mom would love.

Pressed Grilled Vegetable Sandwich

Pressed sandwiches are Cuban creations.
This one calls for an array of grilled vegetables.

1. Preheat an outdoor grill or oven broiler.

2. Place the bell pepper, eggplant, mushroom, and onion in a large bowl. Add the marinade and toss to coat. Let the vegetables marinate at least 15 minutes before placing them on the hot grill or under the broiler. Cook about 5 minutes on each side and remove from heat.

3. Cut the mushroom into ¼-inch slices.

4. On the bottom half of bread, layer the grilled peppers, eggplant, onions, and mushrooms. Top with mozzarella and basil. (If using Basil Paste, spread it on the inside of the remaining slice of bread.) Cover with the top half of the bread.

5. Place the sandwich on a plate and press it down with the clean bottom of a skillet.

6. Heat the oil in small skillet over medium heat. Place the sandwich in the skillet top side down, and heat for 3 to 5 minutes, or until the bread on the bottom is lightly browned. Using a spatula, turn the sandwich over and brown the other side.

7. Remove the sandwich from the skillet, and transfer to a plate. Cut diagonally into triangles and enjoy!

VEGAN CHOICE

• Replace the mozzarella cheese with soy mozzarella.

Yield: 1 sandwich

I small red bell pepper, halved and seeded

I eggplant slice, about 1 inch thick and cut lengthwise

I medium-sized Portabella mushroom cap

I small onion, cut into ¼-inch slices

I recipe Basic Marinade (page 100)

I piece focaccia bread (4-inch square), cut in half horizontally*

I ounce shredded mozzarella cheese

2 tablespoon shredded fresh basil, or 1 tablespoon Basil Paste (page 69)

I tablespoon canola oil

Try making your own focaccia (recipe on page 104), or use a commercial variety.

As-You-Like-It Hoagie

Also known as a hero, submarine, grinder, or poor boy—
depending on what part of the country you're in—
the hoagie is typically a hearty sandwich that
includes any filling that your heart desires.

Yield: 1 sandwich

4-inch-long roll, or piece of
French or Italian bread

2 tablespoons Modern
Mayonnaise (page 64),
or commercial variety

2 ounces thinly sliced
turkey pastrami

2 ounces thinly sliced
prosciutto

2 ounces shredded mozzarella
or Cheddar cheese

3 thin tomato slices

1 cup shredded lettuce

1 tablespoon red wine vinegar

1. Cut the roll in half horizontally. Spread the mayonnaise on the inside part of both halves.

2. Layer the pastrami and prosciutto on the bottom half of the bread. Top with the cheese, tomato slices, and lettuce. Sprinkle with vinegar, then cover with the top half of the roll.

3. Serve with a dill pickle spear or the condiment of your choice.

MEATLESS CHOICE

• Although you can choose any luncheon meat alternative, I recommend replacing the pastrami with sliced vegetarian sausage, and the prosciutto with vegetarian Canadian bacon or ham.

VEGAN CHOICE

• Replace the Modern Mayonnaise with Soy Mayonnaise (page 64), Ginger-Miso Dressing (page 60), or Sesame-Mustard Vinaigrette (page 62).

• Instead of dairy cheese, use soy mozzarella or other soy-based variety.

Judith's DLT

Using the sea vegetable dulse instead of bacon gives this
classic sandwich a new twist. It was the creation of
Judith, my wonderful friend and an inspired cook,
who helped me test the recipes for this book.

1. Preheat a dry 10-inch skillet over medium heat. Add the dulse, and toast it about 2 minutes on one side and 1 minute on the other, or until crisp. (Be careful not to burn it.) Set aside.

2. Toast the bread, then spread one side of each slice with mayonnaise. Set aside.

3. Place the dulse on one of the slices of bread. Top with the tomatoes and lettuce. Cover with the remaining slice of bread.

4. Cut diagonally, and serve with Red Cabbage Slaw (page 52) or the condiment of your choice.

Yield: 1 sandwich

12 pieces (about 1-inch long each) dulse

2 slices whole wheat bread

2 tablespoons Modern Mayonnaise (page 64), or commercial variety

2 large tomato slices

1/2 cup shredded lettuce

VEGAN CHOICE

• Replace the Modern Mayonnaise with Soy Mayonnaise (page 64).

Grilled Cheese and Veggie Sandwich

Here's another delicious way to add interest to an ordinary grilled cheese sandwich.

Yield: 4 sandwiches

8 thin slices zucchini

4 thin slices eggplant

4 thin slices Spanish onion

1 recipe Basic Marinade
(page 100)

8 slices whole wheat bread

8 slices Muenster, Swiss, or
mozzarella cheese

3 teaspoons canola or peanut oil

1. Preheat an outdoor grill or oven broiler.

2. Place the zucchini, eggplant, and onion in a large bowl. Add the marinade and toss to coat. Let the vegetables marinate at least 15 minutes before placing them on the hot grill or under the broiler. Cook about 5 minutes on each side and remove from heat.

3. Lay out four slices of bread. On each, place two slices of zucchini, one slice of eggplant, and one slice of onion. Top each with two slices of cheese. Cover with a slice of bread, and press slightly.

4. Heat the oil in a large skillet over medium heat. Add the sandwiches, and grill for 3 to 5 minutes, or until the bread on the bottom is lightly browned. Using a spatula, turn the sandwiches over, press down slightly with the spatula, and brown the other side.

5. Remove the sandwiches from the skillet, and transfer to a plate. Cut diagonally and serve.

VEGAN CHOICE

- Instead of dairy cheese, use soy mozzarella or other soy-based cheese.

Grilled Cheese and Egg Salad Sandwich

Egg salad is an interesting addition to the run-of-the-mill grilled cheese sandwich.

1. Divide the egg salad between three slices of bread. Top each with cheese, and cover with the remaining bread.

2. Spread the outsides of the sandwiches with butter, and place them in a large skillet over medium heat. Grill for 3 to 5 minutes or until the bread on the bottom is lightly browned. Using a spatula, turn the sandwich over, press down slightly with the spatula, and brown the other side.

3. Remove the sandwich from the skillet, and transfer to a plate. Cut diagonally and serve.

Yield: 3 sandwiches

1 ½ cups Egg Salad (page 59)

6 slices whole grain bread

3 ounces sliced mozzarella or Swiss cheese

7 teaspoons softened butter

VEGAN CHOICE

- Replace the Egg Salad with Tofu "Egg" Salad (page 60).
- Instead of dairy cheese, use soy mozzarella or Swiss.
- Use corn or other vegetable oil in place of butter.

Canadian Bacon, Lettuce, and Tomato Sandwich

Using lean Canadian bacon makes this a healthier version of the classic BLT.

1. Toast the bread, then spread one side of each slice with mayonnaise. Set aside.

2. Heat the oil in a small sauté pan over medium heat. Add the Canadian bacon, and brown about 3 minutes on each side.

3. Place the bacon on one of the slices of bread. Top with the tomatoes and lettuce. Cover with the remaining slice of bread.

4. Cut diagonally, and serve with a dill pickle spear or the condiment of your choice.

MEATLESS CHOICE

• Instead of Canadian bacon, use vegetarian-style Canadian bacon, smoked seitan, or tofu.

VEGAN CHOICE

• Replace the Modern Mayonnaise with Soy Mayonnaise (page 64).

Yield: 1 sandwich

2 slices whole wheat bread

2 tablespoons Modern Mayonnaise (page 64), or commercial variety

2 teaspoons peanut, canola, or extra-virgin olive oil

2 slices Canadian bacon

2 large tomato slices

1/2 cup shredded lettuce

Orange Barbecued Chicken Sandwich

The orange-flavored barbecue sauce helps elevate an ordinary grilled chicken sandwich to new heights.

1. Combine all of the marinade ingredients in a shallow bowl, add the chicken, and turn to coat. Refrigerate for at least 30 minutes.

2. Preheat an oven broiler or an outdoor grill. If using a grill, cook the marinated cutlets for about 5 minutes on each side, or until the chicken is no longer pink inside when cut with a knife. If using an oven broiler, place the cutlets in an oiled casserole dish, and broil 7 to 10 minutes on each side.

3. Thinly slice each cutlet on an angle.

4. Arrange equal portions of sliced chicken on the bottom half of each bun. Top each with two tomato slices, and cover with the top half of the buns.

MEATLESS CHOICE

• Replace the chicken with a vegetarian chicken alternative, such as Chiken Brest by Harvest Direct, or another option. (See choices in Chapter One.)

Yield: 4 sandwiches

4 chicken breast cutlets (about 6 ounces each)

4 toasted whole wheat burger buns

8 tomato slices

MARINADE

5 tablespoons barbecue sauce

$\frac{1}{4}$ cup orange juice concentrate

1 tablespoon molasses

$1\frac{1}{2}$ teaspoons Dijon mustard

1 teaspoon minced fresh garlic

MARINATING FOODS

Marinades are used to preserve foods as well as infuse them with tantalizing flavors. Ingredients for marinades can begin with your favorite wine, citrus juice, or flavored vinegar, and include your choice of spices and herbs.

When meat or poultry is left to marinate, the marinade's acid will act as a tenderizer. However, overmarinating will cause the food to become mushy and fall apart. For this reason, never let meats sit in marinade for more than twenty-four hours. And don't let seafood marinate more than an hour or two, as the acidity will begin to "cook" the fish. When marinating vegetables for long periods of time, be aware that the acidity will cause green varieties to lose their vibrant color.

When meats are grilled, they can create compounds known as heterocyclic aromatic amines (HAAs), which have been shown to cause cancer in monkeys and rats, and possibly in humans. Although steaks, burgers, and bacon are the most common meats linked to HAAs, The National Cancer Institute has shown that grilled chicken can also harbor high levels. But marinating can help reduce these levels. According to a study conducted by The American Chemical Soci-ety, steeping a chicken breast in an acid-based marinade for just five minutes can reduce HAAs by 90 percent.

There are a number of safety precautions to follow when marinating meats, poultry, and sea-food. The following guidelines do not apply when marinating plant-based foods, such as tem-peh, seitan, tofu, and other vegetarian meat alternatives.

☐ Always marinate foods in the refrigerator to prevent bacterial growth.

☐ Do not use raw marinade from the meat or poultry (which may contain bacteria) to baste food as it cooks. If, however, you bring the mari-nade to a rolling boil for at least one minute, it will be safe to use.

☐ Once the food is cooked, transfer it to a clean plate. Don't return it to the unwashed plate in which it had been marinating.

You can use the marinade recipe below for both meats and vegetables. The orange juice ingredient gives it a wonderful citrus flavor. If you are using this marinade with seafood, try substi-tuting the milder rice vinegar for the balsamic.

Yield: About 1¼ cups

½ cup balsamic vinegar

¼ cup olive oil

¼ cup tamari soy sauce (optional)

¼ cup orange juice

¾ teaspoon sea salt

½ teaspoon ground ginger

Basic Marinade

1. Combine all of the ingredients in a mixing bowl and stir well. Set aside until ready to use.

2. If not using immediately, store the marinade in a covered container in the refrigerator, where it will keep for about six months.

Turkey Dijon Sandwich

This sandwich is a great way to use leftover
Turkey Loaf or turkey burgers.

1. Heat 1 teaspoon of the oil in small skillet over medium heat. Add the apple slices, and cook until soft and caramelized. Remove to a plate, and set aside.

2. Heat the remaining oil in the skillet, add the Turkey Loaf, and brown about 3 minutes on each side.

3. Spread the dressing on one slice of bread, then top with the turkey, tomato, lettuce, and apple. Cover with the remaining slice of bread.

4. Cut the sandwich on the diagonal, and serve.

MEATLESS CHOICE

• Use vegetarian option for Turkey Loaf (page 125), or any vegetarian poultry alternative.

Yield: 1 sandwich

2 teaspoons extra-virgin olive oil

4 thin apple slices

1 thick slice Turkey Loaf (page 125), or any leftover cooked turkey or chicken

1 tablespoon Sesame-Mustard Vinaigrette (page 62), or Dijon mustard

2 slices whole wheat bread

2 large tomato slices

$1/2$ cup shredded lettuce

Whole Wheat Honey Beer Bread

When choosing the type of beer to use in this recipe, keep in mind that dark, strong-flavored beers result in darker-colored, stronger-flavored loaves.

1. In a small mixing bowl, proof the yeast by combining it with the warm water and honey. Lightly oil an 8-x-4-inch loaf pan and set aside.

2. In a medium-sized mixing bowl, combine the flours, caraway seeds, and salt, and set aside. In another large bowl, add the oil, yeast mixture, and beer. Slowly add the flour mixture to the wet ingredients, mixing it with your hands or a wooden spoon until it is well combined.

3. Turn the dough onto a floured surface, and knead for a few minutes until it is smooth and slightly elastic.

4. Form the dough into a loaf, and place it in the prepared pan. Brush the top with a little oil to prevent if from forming a crust. Let the dough rise uncovered for 35 to 45 minutes, or until it has doubled in size

5. Bake in a preheated 375°F oven for 30 to 45 minutes, or until the bread is golden brown.

6. Remove the loaf from the pan, and place it on a wire rack. Allow the bread to cool before serving.

Yield: 8-inch loaf

2 packages (1.5 ounces each) active dry yeast

$\frac{1}{2}$ cup warm water

2 teaspoons honey

2 cups whole wheat bread flour

2 cups unbleached white flour

1 tablespoon caraway seeds

2 teaspoons sea salt

3 tablespoons canola oil

1 cup warm beer

VEGAN CHOICE

• Replace the honey with sugar when proofing the yeast in Step 1.

Porter Beer Quick Bread

Great for sandwiches, this quick bread is also a wonderful accompaniment for bean dishes and grilled foods.

1. Preheat the oven to 375°F. Oil and flour a 9-x-5-inch loaf pan, and set aside.

2. In a large mixing bowl, combine the flour, brown sugar, baking powder, and salt. Slowly add the beer, while stirring with a wooden spoon. Mix well.

3. Pour the mixture into the prepared loaf pan, and bake for 35 to 40 minutes, or until golden brown.

4. Remove the loaf from the pan, and place it on a wire rack. Allow the bread to cool before serving.

Yield: 9-inch loaf

3 cups unbleached white flour, or combination 1½ cups whole wheat flour and 1½ cups whole wheat pastry flour

3 tablespoons brown sugar

1 tablespoon baking powder

1½ teaspoons sea salt

12 ounces warm porter beer, or other dark beer

PROOFING YEAST

To insure successful yeast bread, it is necessary to check, or proof, the yeast for freshness. To do this, simply combine the yeast with a half cup or so of warm water. (You can also add a bit of honey.) If the mixture foams within a few minutes, the yeast is active and good to use.

It is also important that the water used for proofing, as well as any liquid that is called for in the recipe, is warm—preferably between 110°F and 115°F. Water that is too hot will kill the yeast, while cold water will prevent it from activating properly.

Focaccia

*This wonderful Italian flatbread is great for sandwiches
and is surprisingly easy to make.*

Yield: Two 12-inch-square flatbreads

1 package (1.5 ounces) active
dry yeast

1½ cups warm water

2 teaspoons honey

1¾ cups unbleached white flour

1½ cups stone-ground whole
wheat bread flour

2 tablespoons extra-virgin olive oil

2 teaspoons garlic powder

1. In a small mixing bowl, proof the yeast by combining it with ¼ cup of the warm water and the honey. Lightly oil two medium-sized baking sheets, and set aside.

2. In a medium-sized mixing bowl, combine the flours, and set aside. In a large mixing bowl, add the oil, the yeast mixture, and the remaining water, and mix well. Slowly add the flour mixture to the wet ingredients, mixing it with your hands until it is well combined.

3. Turn the dough onto a floured surface, and knead for a few minutes until it is smooth and slightly elastic.

4. Form the dough into a ball, and place it in a large bowl that has been coated with oil. Turn the dough over in the bowl to coat it with oil on all sides. Cover the bowl with a clean damp cloth, and set it in a warm place for about 45 minutes, or until the dough has doubled in size.

5. With a floured fist, punch down the risen dough, and knead it for about 2 minutes. Divide the dough in half, and place on the prepared baking sheets. Using your fingertips, press each piece into a 12-inch square, about ¼-inch thick. To minimize air bubbles, poke holes in the dough with a fork at 1-inch intervals.

6. Brush the surface of each square of dough with olive oil and sprinkle with garlic powder; then place in a preheated 350°F oven for about 20 minutes, or until the crust is golden brown.

7. Remove and let cool before serving. (You can partially bake the crusts about 8 minutes, allow to cool, and freeze them for use at a later time.)

VEGAN CHOICE

• Eliminate the honey when proofing the yeast in Step 1.

7

Tantalizing Seafood, Meat, and Poultry Entrées

Cooking for people with diverse taste preferences can be very challenging, especially when it comes to preparing the entrée. An entrée is a meal's centerpiece. For many, a meal just isn't a meal without a traditional dish that includes seafood, poultry, or meat. However, a growing number of people, are joining the vegetarian movement and opting for non-meat meals. Although this may seem like a daunting task for the harried cook, you'll be glad to know that help is just a page or two away.

This chapter presents a wealth of popular entrées that, with a few easy ingredient adjustments, can help you meet the challenge of preparing meals for meat- as well as non-meat-eaters. Included are seafood entrées such as spicy Shrimp Creole, poultry classics such as lemony Chicken Piccata, and mouth-watering meat dishes like Beef Stroganoff. And each and every dish, either prepared traditionally or with creative vegetarian options, is a sure-fire winner. Without a doubt, once you try these recipes, you 're gonna love 'em!

Crab Corn Cakes

*My friend Alfonso Contrisciani gave me this recipe,
which I modified a bit.*

1. Heat 1 tablespoon of the oil in a 12-inch sauté pan over medium heat. Add the bell peppers, onions, corn, and thyme, and sauté for 10 to 15 minutes, or until the peppers are soft and the onions are transparent. Transfer the mixture to a baking sheet, and spread it out to cool. Blot any excess moisture with paper towels.

2. In a large mixing bowl, combine the mayonnaise, mustard, Worcestershire sauce, Tabasco sauce, and eggs. Add the sautéed vegetables and crab meat. Mix well.

3. In a separate mixing bowl, add the Old Bay seasoning to the bread crumbs, and combine well. Add the crumbs to the crab mixture, and mix until well combined.

4. Form ¼-cup portions of the mixture into 16 patties. To make 32 appetizer-sized cakes, use 2-tablespoon portions.

5. Heat the remaining 2 teaspoons of oil in the sauté pan over medium-low heat. When the oil is hot, add the cakes. Cook for 3 to 5 minutes, or until the bottom of the cakes are brown. Using a spatula, carefully turn them over, and continue to cook another 2 to 3 minutes, or until browned on the second side.

6. Serve immediately.

VEGAN CHOICE

- The Sea Vegetable Corn Cakes on page 152 offer a vegan version of this recipe.

Yield: 16 cakes
(about 3 inches),
or 32 appetizer-sized cakes

1 tablespoon plus 2 teaspoons canola oil

2 cups finely diced red bell peppers

2 cups finely diced green bell peppers

1¼ cups finely diced onion

1 cup cooked whole kernel corn (canned or frozen/thawed varieties are fine)

½ teaspoon dry thyme

1 cup Modern Mayonnaise (page 64), or commercial variety

3 tablespoons Dijon mustard

1 tablespoon Worcestershire sauce

½ teaspoon Tabasco sauce

3 beaten eggs

1 pound canned or frozen chopped crab meat, drained well

2 tablespoons Old Bay seasoning

2 cups bread crumbs

Salmon Niçoise

Be prepared to receive rave reviews for this simple yet elegant salmon-lover's favorite. As an added bonus, if the Sauce Niçoise is already made, you can have this dish on the table in twenty to thirty minutes.

1. Heat the oil in a 10-inch skillet over medium heat. Place the salmon in the pan skin side up, and brown for 4 to 5 minutes. Using a spatula, carefully turn the salmon over.

2. Pour the wine and Niçoise sauce over the salmon, and continue to cook another 6 to 10 minutes, or until the fish is opaque and easily flakes with a fork.

3. Serve immediately.

Yield: 2 servings

2 teaspoons extra-virgin olive oil

2 salmon fillets with skin (about 6 ounces each)

¼ cup white wine

¾ cup Sauce Niçoise (page 82)

VEGAN CHOICE

- Prepare the Sauce Niçoise without anchovies.
- Instead of salmon, form oval-shaped patties out of uncooked Sea Vegetable Tofu mixture (page 137). After browning the patties, remove them from the pan and set aside. Combine the wine with the Sauce Niçoise and heat up. Spoon the hot sauce onto the plates, and top with the browned "salmon" patties.

Scallops au Gratin

*This seafood dish merges traditional fare
with natural foods ingredients.*

1. Preheat the oven broiler.

2. Warm the butter in a 10-inch ovenproof sauté pan (one with a metal handle) over medium heat. Add the scallops, and sauté for about 3 minutes, then add the wine. Continue sautéing for about 5 minutes, or until the liquid is reduced by about half.

3. While the scallops are sautéing, warm the oil in 2-quart pot over medium heat. Add the spinach, cover, and cook for 1 to 2 minutes, or until it wilts. Set aside.

4. Add the Béchamel Sauce and salt to the sautéed scallops, and cook for an additional 3 minutes. Top with the au gratin mixture, and place under the broiler for 2 to 4 minutes, or until the topping browns.

5. Divide the spinach between two dinner plates. Top with the scallop mixture and serve.

Yield: 2 servings

2 tablespoons butter

8 ounces bay scallops

1/4 cup white wine

2 teaspoons canola oil

4 cups fresh spinach

1/2 cup Béchamel Sauce (page 81), or other white sauce variety

1/4 teaspoon sea salt

1/4 cup Coconut au Gratin Topping (page 72), or a mixture of 3 tablespoons whole wheat bread crumbs, 2 tablespoons unsweetened flaked coconut, 2 tablespoons softened butter, 2 teaspoons minced fresh parsley, and 1 teaspoon minced fresh garlic

VEGAN CHOICE

- Use 4 teaspoons canola oil instead of butter for sautéing.

- Replace the scallops with Sea Vegetable Tofu (page 137) that has been cut into scallop-shaped pieces.

- Use the vegan version of the Coconut au Gratin mixture (page 72), or use soy margarine instead of butter if preparing the gratin mixture presented in the ingredient list above.

A WORD ABOUT FISH

If you enjoy fish, and it is a regular part of your diet, you may be interested to know that it is a healthful choice as well. The omega-3 fatty acids that fish provide have been found to help lower cholesterol, reduce blood pressure, and prevent blood clots.

Seafood is highly perishable, and you should always select the freshest available. The following recommendations for purchasing and preparing fish will help ensure freshness and good taste.

Shopping Guidelines

☐ Let your nose help guide you to the freshest fish, which should have a clean seaweed smell—not a "fishy" odor.

☐ When purchasing fish fillets, make sure the flesh is firm and springy when touched. It should also be translucent.

☐ When purchasing whole fish, choose those with clear eyes, not cloudy ones that are sunken. Look for scales that are shiny and tightly packed, and gills that are bright red rather than dull brown. Finally, take a look at the tail; if it's dried, the fish is probably past its prime.

☐ When buying shrimp, which is often frozen, choose varieties that are gray or white in color. Frozen shrimp that is pink has already been cooked and is likely to have lost most of its flavor.

☐ Watch out for shrimp that smells like ammonia—it's a sure sign of spoilage.

☐ Choose scallops that are fresh-smelling and firm. Like shrimp, an ammonia-like smell indicates spoilage.

☐ When possible, choose fish that live in deep waters far out at sea, such as cod, flounder, and halibut. Avoid coastal and freshwater fish, such as bass, swordfish, catfish, and trout, which are fatty and are more likely to accumulate toxins from contaminated water.

Preparation Guidelines

☐ Refrigerate fresh fish immediately and cover it with ice if possible. Cook it the same day it is purchased or shortly after.

☐ Fish cooks quickly; however, cooking times will vary depending on the thickness of the fish and the cooking temperature. You'll know the fish is cooked when its flesh is opaque and easily flakes with a fork.

☐ Don't overcook fish or other seafood. When overdone, fish dries out quickly and becomes tasteless; shrimp and scallops become hard and rubbery.

Balsamic Demi-Glace Chicken
with Polenta (page 117)
[TOP LEFT]

Turkey Fricassee (page 124)
[TOP RIGHT]

Moo Goo Gai Pan (page 119)
[BOTTOM]

Beef Pepper Steak Pasta (page 130)
[TOP RIGHT]

Barbecued Pork (page 133)
and Carrot Cornbread (page 34)
[TOP LEFT]

Beef Schnitzel (page 131)
[BOTTOM]

Coconut au Gratin Shrimp

This was always a favorite seafood dish of mine.
It is simple to prepare and will delight seafood lovers.

1. Preheat the oven to 375°F. Lightly oil a 1½-quart casserole dish and set aside.

2. In a large mixing bowl, combine the shrimp and 1½ cups of the gratin mixture. Transfer the shrimp to the casserole dish, pour the wine evenly on top, then sprinkle with the remaining gratin.

3. Bake uncovered for 15 to 20 minutes, or until the shrimp turn pink and are tender.

4. Serve hot over rice.

Yield:
4 to 6 servings

2 pounds shrimp, deveined

1 recipe Coconut au Gratin Topping (page 72)

½ cup white wine

VEGAN CHOICE

• Replace the shrimp with appetizer-sized portions of Sea Vegetable Tofu (page 137).

• Use the vegan version of the gratin mixture (page 72).

Shrimp Creole

The sauce used in this recipe will take on
the flavor of the shrimp.

1. Heat the oil in a large skillet over medium heat. Add the shrimp, and lightly sauté, tossing gently, for 3 to 5 minutes.

2. Add the remaining ingredients, stirring well to combine. Heat thoroughly for 10 minutes, allowing the flavors of the herbs and spices to permeate the shrimp.

3. Serve hot over rice.

VEGAN CHOICE

• Replace the shrimp with appetizer-sized portions of Sea Vegetable Tofu (page 137).

Halibut Spring Rolls

Sealing the fish in a spring roll wrapper holds it together during the cooking process.

1. Preheat the oven to 350°F.

2. In a small sauté pan over medium heat, add the mushrooms, spinach, and salt. Sauté until the spinach wilts, then immediately remove the pan from the heat.

3. If using dried spring roll wrappers, place them on a large dinner plate that is covered with water, and let them sit for about 1 minute, or until they are soft.

4. Place one of the softened wrappers on a clean work surface. Overlap the second wrapper over the bottom third of the first wrapper, and spoon the spinach-mushroom mixture across the middle. Top with the halibut. Close the wrapper around the fish, as you would wrap a package, then turn it over seal side down for a moment.

5. Heat the oil in the sauté pan over medium heat. Place the fish "packet" seal side down in the hot pan, and cook for 5 to 7 minutes, or until the bottom of the wrapper is brown. Using a spatula, carefully turn the packet over and cook another 5 minutes.

6. Place the package seal side down on a baking sheet or in a casserole dish, and bake for 10 to 15 minutes.

7. Transfer the fish packet to a plate, and slice in half on a 45-degree angle. Enjoy hot with your favorite sauce. Hollandaise Sauce (page 68) is recommended.

Yield: 1 serving

1 tablespoon sliced Shiitake mushrooms

1/4 cup chopped fresh spinach, or 2 tablespoons frozen and thawed

Pinch sea salt

2 spring roll wrappers (6-inch squares)*

1 skinless, boneless halibut steak (about 6 ounces)

1 teaspoon canola oil

* These wrappers come either in dried sheets, which need to be soaked and softened before using, or in convenient ready-to-use squares, which are found in the refrigerator section of most supermarkets.

VEGAN CHOICE

- Replace the halibut with ½ cup of uncooked Sea Vegetable Tofu mixture (page 137).
- If using Hollandaise Sauce, use the vegan version on page 68.

Poached Halibut

*Poaching—gently simmering food in a small amount
of water or seasoned liquid—is a traditional
and classic way to cook seafood.*

Yield: 4 servings

2 cups water

I cup thinly sliced onions

$\frac{1}{2}$ cup thinly sliced carrots

$\frac{1}{2}$ cup thinly sliced celery

I $\frac{1}{2}$ teaspoons sea salt

$\frac{1}{8}$ teaspoon dry thyme

I bay leaf

2 tablespoons Roux (page 86),
or 2 tablespoons flour mixed
with I tablespoon canola oil

$\frac{1}{4}$ cup whole milk or cream

$\frac{1}{4}$ cup white wine

4 skinless, boneless halibut steaks
(about 4 ounces each)

$\frac{1}{4}$ cup sliced leeks (optional)

1. In a 2-quart saucepan over medium-low heat, add the water, onions, carrots, celery, sea salt, thyme, and bay leaf. Simmer the vegetables, covered, for about 20 minutes. Add the wine, increase the heat, and bring to a boil.

2. Add the fish, cover, and reduce the heat to low. Poach for 5 to 7 minutes, or until the fish is opaque and can be easily flaked with a fork. Transfer the fish to a plate, and cover to keep warm.

3. Strain the broth into another small saucepan, and place it over medium heat. Add the leeks and roux, stirring constantly until the mixture begins to thicken. Stir in the milk.

4. Place some of the sauce on four individual dinner plates, top with the poached fish, then drape with additional sauce. Serve immediately.

VEGAN CHOICE

- Use soy milk in place of the whole milk.
- Instead of halibut, form four oval-shaped "fillets" out of uncooked Sea Vegetable Tofu mixture (page 137). Simmer the fillets in the sauce for 5 to 7 minutes.

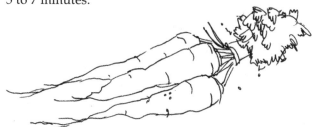

Chicken Piccata

Try this dish, which is one of my favorites, over spaghetti, orzo pasta, or rice pilaf. If the sauce is too strong for your taste, add 1 teaspoon of sugar to reduce the tartness. Or you can decrease the lemon juice by 2 tablespoons and replace it with 2 tablespoons of white wine.

1. To make the sauce, heat the butter in a saucepan over medium heat. Add the onions and garlic, and sauté for 5 to 7 minutes, or until the onions are soft. Gradually add the flour, stirring constantly until it is totally dissolved.

2. Add the broth, continuing to stir until the mixture becomes thick. Stir in the wine and lemon juice.

3. Pour half of the sauce in a blender, and pulse three or four times. Add the remaining sauce, and blend on medium speed until smooth. Cover and let sit for a minute.

4. Dredge the chicken cutlets in the flour and set aside. Heat the oil in a 10- or 12-inch sauté pan over medium heat. Add the chicken, and cook for about 5 to 7 minutes, or until the bottoms are brown. Turn the chicken, and continue to cook for 3 to 5 minutes, or until the second sides are browned. Transfer the cooked cutlets to a plate that is lined with paper towels to absorb any excess oil.

5. Return the sauce to the pan, add the capers and salt, and heat up over medium-low heat.

6. Serve the chicken hot, drizzled with the sauce.

Yield: 4 servings

1½ pounds thinly sliced chicken breast cutlets

¼ cup unbleached white flour

1 tablespoon extra-virgin olive oil

SAUCE

1 tablespoon butter

2½ cups chopped Spanish onions

1 tablespoon minced fresh garlic

¼ cup unbleached white flour

1 cup chicken broth

¾ cup white wine

¼ cup lemon juice

2 tablespoons capers

1 teaspoon sea salt

VEGAN CHOICE

- Replace the chicken cutlets with seitan, tempeh, extra-firm regular tofu, or a vegetarian chicken alternative. (See choices in Chapter One.)
- Instead of butter, use extra-virgin olive oil in the sauce.
- Use vegetable broth instead of chicken broth in the sauce.

Chicken Niçoise

*Leftovers of this chicken make
a good topping for a lunch salad.*

Yield: 4 servings

2 tablespoons extra-virgin
olive oil

4 boneless, skinless
chicken breasts
(about 6 ounces each)

$^1/_2$ cup white wine

1 $^3/_4$ cups Sauce Niçoise
(page 82)

1. Heat the oil in a 12-inch skillet over medium heat. Add the chicken, cover, and brown for about 5 minutes. Turn the chicken over.

2. Pour the wine and the Niçoise sauce over the chicken. Cover and continue to cook for another 8 to 12 minutes, or until the chicken is no longer pink inside when cut with a knife.

3. Serve hot.

MEATLESS CHOICE

- Replace the chicken with slices of extra-firm tofu, or a vegetarian chicken alternative. (See choices in Chapter One).

- Prepare the Sauce Niçoise without the anchovies.

Balsamic Demi-Glace Chicken with Polenta

This very special entrée is an excellent choice
when you're having guests for dinner.

1. To make the polenta, bring the water to boil in a 2-quart pot over high heat. Reduce the heat to medium, and add the cornmeal in a slow, steady stream while stirring with a wooden spoon. Add the salt and saffron. Simmer the ingredients, stirring occasionally, for 10 to 15 minutes, or until the mixture thickens. Sprinkle the flour on top and immediately stir it into the mixture.

2. Transfer the mixture to an oiled 8-x-12-inch baking dish, spread it evenly, and cover with plastic wrap. Refrigerate for at least 30 minutes.

3. Preheat the oven to 350°F. Cut the cooled polenta into 12 equal pieces, and warm in the oven for 15 minutes.

4. While the polenta is warming, heat 2 tablespoons of the oil in a 10-inch skillet over medium heat. Add the chicken slices, sprinkle with salt, and sauté about 5 minutes, or until the bottoms are lightly brown. Turn over and cook another 3 minutes, or until the chicken is no longer pink inside. Transfer the chicken to a plate and set aside.

5. Add remaining oil to skillet, toss in spinach, and heat for a few minutes. Heat the Balsamic Demi-Glace in a separate saucepan.

6. Arrange two pieces of warmed polenta on a plate. Place two slices of chicken on top, spoon ¼ cup of demi-glace over chicken. Top with spinach.

Yield: 6 servings

4 tablespoons canola oil

12 slices (2 ounces each) boneless chicken breast

¼ teaspoon sea salt

12-ounce package frozen spinach, thawed and drained

1½ cups Balsamic Demi-Glace (page 83)

POLENTA*

4½ cups water

3 cups cornmeal

1½ teaspoons sea salt

Pinch saffron, optional

¼ cup unbleached white flour

* For added flavor, include 1 cup diced leeks, 2 teaspoons minced garlic, and ½ teaspoon ground fennel to the cornmeal as it cooks.

MEATLESS CHOICE

- Replace the chicken with sliced seitan, tempeh, or a vegetarian chicken alternative. (See choices in Chapter One.)

- In place of the chicken, sometimes I simply double up on the spinach.

Chicken Napoleon

*Most people think of Napoleons as flaky layers of puff pastry
that are separated by rich Bavarian cream and fruit.
These days, Napoleons have slipped into savory cuisine.
And the recipe below is a splendid example.*

Yield: 4 servings

2 tablespoons canola or sesame oil

12 egg roll skins (4-inch squares)

1 1/2 pounds boneless
chicken breasts with skin

1 tablespoon Southwestern Rub
(page 122), optional

1/2 cup water

2 cups carrots, cut into
1/4-inch-thick rounds

2 cups fresh asparagus, trimmed
and cut into 1 1/2-inch pieces

2 cups zucchini, cut into
1/4-inch-thick rounds

1 cup diced red bell pepper

1 cup thinly sliced celery,
or fresh fennel

1 teaspoon dry tarragon

2 tablespoons powdered
chicken bouillon

2 cups Onion-Garlic
Cream Sauce (page 79)

1 cup diced fresh tomatoes
for garnish

Chopped parsley for garnish

1. Heat 1 tablespoon of the oil in a 12-inch skillet over medium heat. Add the egg roll skins, and lightly brown about 20 to 30 seconds on each side. Transfer the skins to a plate that is lined with paper towels to absorb any excess oil.

2. Place the chicken breasts in the skillet skin side down, and brown for about 5 minutes. (If using the rub mixture, remove the skin from the chicken, then rub the spices onto the surface of the chicken before sautéing.) Add the water, cover, and cook the chicken for 15 minutes, or until it is no longer pink inside when cut with a knife.

3. Transfer the chicken to a cutting board and allow it to cool for 10 to 15 minutes. When the chicken is cool enough to handle, remove and discard the skin, then cut it into small chunks. Set aside.

4. Heat the remaining tablespoon of oil in the skillet over medium heat. Add the carrots and sauté for 5 minutes, then add the asparagus, zucchini, bell pepper, celery, tarragon, and chicken bouillon. Sauté for about 5 minutes, or until the vegetables begin to soften. Add the Onion-Garlic Cream Sauce, and warm thoroughly.

5. For each individual serving, place an egg roll skin on a plate, and top with some of the vegetable mixture and 1 or 2 slices of chicken. Cover with another egg roll skin, and repeat the process, topping the stack with a third skin. Garnish with tomatoes and a sprinkling of parsley before serving.

MEATLESS CHOICE

- Replace the chicken with extra-firm tofu, tempeh, seitan, or a vegetarian chicken alternative, such as Chiken Brest by Harvest Direct. (See other choices in Chapter One.)
- Use vegetarian chicken base instead of regular chicken bouillon.

VEGAN CHOICE

- Use the vegan preparation method for the Onion-Garlic Cream Sauce.

Moo Goo Gai Pan

The ginger-garlic combination adds superb flavor to this chicken dish, which also works well with shrimp. Best served over a bed of rice.

1. Heat the oil in a wok or large deep skillet over medium-high heat. Add the chicken and stir-fry about 3 minutes, or until lightly browned.

2. Add the vegetables, and continue to stir-fry for 3 to 5 minutes, or until the vegetables are tender-crisp. Add the sauce and simmer.

3. Serve immediately over rice.

VEGAN CHOICE

- Replace the chicken with ½-inch cubes of extra-firm tofu that have been sprinkled with tamari or other soy sauce. You can also replace the chicken with seitan or a vegetarian chicken alternative. (See choices in Chapter One.)

Yield: 4 servings

1 tablespoon sesame oil

1 pound thinly sliced chicken breast

2 cups thinly sliced onions

2 cups quartered mushrooms

2 cups thinly sliced red and/or green bell peppers

2 cups thinly sliced Napa cabbage

1 cup thinly sliced bok choy

1 cup mung bean sprouts

1 cup sliced water chestnuts

2 cups Moo Goo Gai Pan Sauce (page 86)

Chicken Cacciatore

Cacciatore is the Italian word for "hunter."
Originally, it referred to a dish that contained tomatoes,
onions, and whatever game was caught that day.
The longer this dish sits the more flavorful it becomes.

Yield: 4 servings

¼ cup unbleached white flour

½ teaspoon sea salt

I pound boneless chicken breast,
cut into bite-sized pieces, or a
quartered 2-pound chicken

2 tablespoons extra-virgin olive oil

2 cups diced onions

I cup quartered button mushrooms

I cup diced green bell peppers

2 tablespoons minced fresh garlic

5 teaspoons Italian spice blend,
or a blend of 2 teaspoons basil,
1½ teaspoons oregano, and
1½ teaspoons marjoram

1½ teaspoons sea salt

1½ cups water

I can (12 ounces) tomato paste

½ cup red wine

Chopped parsley for garnish

1. Preheat the oven to 350°F.

2. In a large mixing bowl, combine the flour and salt. Dredge the chicken in the flour mixture.

3. Heat the oil in a 12-inch skillet over medium heat. Add the chicken and cook about 5 minutes on each side until it is begins to brown. Remove from the skillet and set aside.

4. Add the onions, mushrooms, bell peppers, garlic, Italian spice blend, and salt to the skillet. Sauté, stirring occasionally, for 5 minutes, or until the vegetables begin to soften. Add the water, tomato paste, and wine, and stir well.

5. Place the chicken in an ovenproof casserole dish. Pour or ladle the tomato-vegetable sauce on top. Cover and bake in the oven for 30 minutes, or until the chicken is no longer pink inside when cut with a knife.

6. Spoon the hot cacciatore over pasta or rice, and garnish with a sprinkling of chopped parsley.

MEATLESS CHOICE

• Replace the chicken with ½-inch cubes extra-firm tofu or a vegetarian chicken alternative, such as Chiken Nuggets or Chiken Brest by Harvest Direct. (See other choices in Chapter One.) When using one of these meatless alternatives, you can skip the oven baking. Simply add the tofu or other ingredient to the skillet with the tomato sauce, cover and simmer for 5 minutes, then turn off the heat and let stand for 10 minutes.

• For enhanced flavor, add 1 tablespoon vegetarian chicken bouillon or Vogue Vegetable Base to the flour mixture.

Chicken Dijon

*This super quick dish is a variation
of one of my favorite tempeh recipes.*

1. Heat the oil in a 12-inch skillet over medium heat. Add the chicken and cook for 3 to 5 minutes, or until the bottom is lightly browned. (If using the rub mixture, rub it onto the surface of the chicken before cooking.) Turn the chicken over, add the onions, and continue to cook for about 5 minutes, or until the onions are soft and transparent.

2. As the chicken and onions cook, steam the cabbage and set it aside.

3. Combine the mustard, miso, and 1 cup of the water in a mixing bowl. Add to the skillet, stir well, and simmer uncovered for 5 to 7 minutes.

4. Mix the cornstarch with the remaining tablespoon of water, then add it to the skillet, stirring well, until the sauce thickens.

5. To serve, spoon some sauce on a dinner plate. Top first with the chicken and onions, and then with the cabbage.

Yield: 3 servings

1 tablespoon sesame oil

3 chicken cutlets
(about 4 ounces each)

1 tablespoon American Rub
(page 122), optional

2 cups sliced onions

2 cups shredded green cabbage,
preferably Napa or Savoy

2 tablespoons Dijon mustard

2 tablespoons mellow
white miso

1 cup plus 1 tablespoon water

1 tablespoon cornstarch

MEATLESS CHOICE

• Replace the chicken with extra-firm tofu, tempeh, seitan, or a vegetarian chicken alternative, such as Chiken Brest by Harvest Direct. (See other choices in Chapter One.)

FLAVORFUL SEASONING RUBS

When a seasoning rub is added to the surface of meat, seafood, or poultry, it imparts a unique burst of flavor—without any fat or salt. Use your fingers to rub the dry blend onto the food's outer surface, then allow the spices to permeate the food for at least fifteen minutes before cooking. I don't recommend grilling foods that have been "rubbed," because the intense heat of the grill can burn the spices, making them bitter. Roasting is recommended. You can also add rub mixtures to burgers to enhance their flavor.

Stored in airtight containers, the following rubs will remain flavorful for many months, so make a few batches to always have some on hand.

American Rub

Yield: About 3 tablespoons
(will cover approximately
3 pounds of meat or poultry)

1 tablespoon rosemary

1 teaspoon thyme

1 teaspoon dry mustard

1 teaspoon sea salt

½ teaspoon ground black pepper

2 tablespoons unbleached white flour

1. Place the rosemary, thyme, mustard, salt, and pepper in a clean coffee grinder* and pulverize to a fine powder.

2. Transfer to a bowl, add the flour, and mix well.

3. Apply the rub as directed above.

Southwestern Rub

Yield: About 6 tablespoons
(will cover approximately
6 pounds of meat or poultry)

1 tablespoon cumin

1 tablespoon chili powder

1 tablespoon garlic powder

2 teaspoons sea salt

2 tablespoons unbleached white flour

1. Place all of the ingredients in a small bowl, and mix well.

2. Apply the rub as directed above.

* Be sure the grinder you use is for seasonings only. (If it has been used for grinding coffee beans, the coffee flavor will permeate the rub mix.) You can also use a mortar and pestle to crush the seasonings. Or, at the very least, put the spices in a bowl and crush them with the backside of a spoon.

Orange Barbecued Chicken

This chicken dish has an unusual yet delectable blend of flavors.

1. In a mixing bowl, combine all of the marinade ingredients and mix well. Add the chicken and toss to evenly coat.

2. Marinate the chicken in the refrigerator for at least 30 minutes, although 2 to 3 hours is preferred.

3. You can either barbecue the chicken on a hot outdoor grill, or cook it in an oven broiler. If using a grill, cook the chicken about 5 minutes on each side, or until it is no longer pink inside when cut with a knife. If using the broiler, place the chicken in a casserole dish along with the marinade and cook for 15 to 20 minutes, turning and basting every 5 minutes or so.

4. Serve hot with garlic mashed potatoes and a fresh vegetable.

Yield: 4 servings

4 boneless chicken breasts
(about 6 ounces each)

MARINADE

$\frac{1}{4}$ cup orange juice concentrate

$\frac{1}{4}$ cup barbecue sauce

$4\frac{1}{2}$ teaspoons tamari
or other soy sauce

1 tablespoon molasses

1 teaspoon Dijon mustard

1 teaspoon lemon juice

1 teaspoon minced
fresh garlic

MEATLESS CHOICE

- Replace the chicken with 4 pieces firm tofu, or a vegetarian chicken alternative such as Chiken Brest by Harvest Direct. (See other choices in Chapter One.)

Turkey Fricassee

*Traditionally, after Thanksgiving, I look forward to making
this dish from leftover turkey. It is one of my favorites,
and easily works with leftover chicken, too.
I serve it alongside mashed potatoes.*

Yield: 4 servings

2 tablespoons butter

¹/₂ cup diced onions

¹/₂ cup diced red bell pepper

¹/₂ cup diced green bell pepper

I cup peeled, thinly sliced carrots

3 tablespoons chicken bouillon

I teaspoon minced fresh garlic

¹/₂ teaspoon sea salt

¹/₈ teaspoon white pepper

¹/₄ cup unbleached white flour

2 cups chicken or turkey broth

2 cups cooked turkey,
cut into bite-sized cubes

¹/₂ cup ¹/₄-inch celery slices

¹/₂ cup fresh or frozen peas

2 tablespoons sherry wine

1. Heat the butter in a skillet over medium heat. Add the onions, bell peppers, carrots, chicken bouillon, garlic, salt, and pepper. Sauté, stirring occasionally, for about 5 minutes, or until the vegetables begin to soften and the onions are transparent.

2. Stir the flour into the mixture and cook for another 2 minutes.

3. While stirring, add the broth one cup at a time. Then add the turkey, celery, peas, and wine. Continue to cook for about 5 minutes, or until the vegetables are hot but still tender-crisp.

4. Serve hot alongside or on top of plain rice or mashed potatoes.

MEATLESS CHOICE

- Use canola oil instead of butter.
- Instead of chicken bouillon, use vegetarian chicken or vegetable bouillon.
- Use vegetable broth in place of the turkey or chicken broth.
- Replace the turkey with ¹/₂-inch cubes of extra-firm tofu or a vegetarian chicken alternative. (See choices in Chapter One).

Turkey Loaf

This is a great way to combine tofu with ground turkey,
chicken, or beef. The tofu acts as a binder.
Try it with the Velouté Sauce (page 87).

1. Preheat the oven to 375°F. Oil a 9-x-4-inch loaf pan, and set aside.

2. Heat the sesame oil in a 12-inch skillet over medium heat. Add the turkey, onions, celery, carrots, garlic, poultry seasoning, thyme, basil, and salt. Mix well and sauté, stirring occasionally, until the vegetables are very soft and the turkey is no longer pink. (If the turkey is very lean, add another tablespoon or two of oil to the skillet.)

3. Remove the skillet from the heat, stir in the flour and the Tofu Pâté, and mix well.

4. Transfer the mixture to the loaf pan, and bake in the oven for 30 to 40 minutes, or until the top is lightly browned and the loaf is firm to the touch. Remove from the oven.

5. Run a dull knife along the sides of the pan, then invert it onto a serving plate to release the loaf. Let sit about 5 minutes before slicing and serving.

MEATLESS CHOICE

- Replace the ground turkey with 1 pound rehydrated TVP (1 cup dry TVP with 2 cups hot water and 1 tablespoon vegetarian bouillon).

- Or replace the ground turkey with a 15-ounce can of drained kidney beans.

Yield: 9-x-4-inch loaf

1 tablespoon sesame oil

1 pound ground turkey

1 cup finely diced onions

1 cup finely diced celery

1 cup shredded carrots

1 tablespoon minced fresh garlic

1 teaspoon poultry seasoning

1 teaspoon dry thyme

1 teaspoon dry basil

1 teaspoon sea salt

1/4 cup unbleached white flour

2 cups Tofu Pâté (page 141),
or smooth blend of 2 cups
crumbled tofu,
4 1/2 teaspoons arrowroot,
1 tablespoon sesame oil,
1 teaspoon agar powder,
and 1/4 teaspoon sea salt

Favorite Meat Loaf

As American as apple pie, meat loaf is one of those dishes that can be converted easily into a meatless meal.

Yield: 8-x-4-inch loaf

2 tablespoons sesame oil

1 ½ cups finely diced onions

1 cup shredded carrots

2 teaspoons minced
fresh garlic

1 teaspoon dry savory

1 teaspoon dry whole thyme

½ teaspoon sea salt

¼ cup bulghur wheat

1 pound lean ground beef

1 beaten egg

1. Preheat the oven to 350°F. Oil an 8-x-4-inch loaf pan, and set aside.

2. Heat the oil in a 12-inch skillet over medium heat. Add the onions, carrots, garlic, savory, thyme, and salt. Sauté for about 3 minutes, or until the vegetables begin to soften. Add the bulghur and cook for another 3 minutes. Remove from the heat and set aside.

3. In a large mixing bowl, combine the ground beef and egg. Add the sautéed vegetable mixture, and mix by hand until well combined.

4. Transfer the mixture to the loaf pan, and bake in the oven for 30 to 40 minutes, or until the top is lightly browned and the loaf is firm to the touch. Remove from the oven.

5. Run a dull knife along the sides of the pan, then invert it onto a serving plate to release the loaf. Let sit about 5 minutes before slicing and serving.

MEATLESS CHOICE

• Replace the ground beef with 12 ounces rehydrated TVP (³⁄₄ cup dry TVP with 1½ cups hot water and 2 teaspoons vegetarian beef bouillon).

VEGAN CHOICE

• Replace the egg with 2 tablespoons flax meal.

Salisbury Steak

Kind of an "upscale" hamburger, Salisbury steak is covered with a savory brown sauce and baked in the oven.

1. Preheat the oven to 350°F.

2. Heat 1 tablespoon of the oil in a 12-inch sauté pan over medium heat. Add the onions, mushrooms, garlic, basil, thyme, and salt. Sauté 5 to 7 minutes, or until onions are soft and transparent. Remove from the heat and set aside.

3. In a large mixing bowl, combine the ground beef and egg. Add the bread crumbs and sautéed vegetable mixture, and mix by hand until well combined. Form the mixture into 6 oval-shaped patties.

4. Heat the remaining tablespoon of oil in the sauté pan over medium heat. Add the patties and brown the bottoms for 3 to 5 minutes. Using a spatula, turn the patties over, and brown the other side for another 3 minutes.

5. Transfer the cooked patties to a baking dish, and top with the sauce. Cover and bake for 20 to 30 minutes, or until the "steaks" are cooked.

6. Serve hot with creamy mashed potatoes.

Yield: 6 servings

2 tablespoons canola
or sesame oil

I cup finely diced onions

I cup finely diced mushrooms

I tablespoon minced fresh garlic

I teaspoon dry basil

I teaspoon dry thyme

I teaspoon sea salt

I pound ground beef

I beaten egg

½ cup bread crumbs

3 cups French Brown Sauce
(page 80),
or other brown sauce variety

MEATLESS CHOICE

• A meatless version of this dish is presented on page 153.

Chili Mac

*This hot and hearty dish is perfect to serve
on cold winter days.*

1 cup elbow macaroni
or small shell pasta

1 tablespoon canola or sesame oil

12 ounces lean ground beef

2 cups diced onions

1 cup diced celery

1 cup diced green bell pepper

¼ cup minced fresh garlic

4 teaspoons chili powder

2 teaspoons cumin powder

1 tablespoon tamari
or other soy sauce

1 can (15 ounces) kidney beans,
drained

4 cups diced canned tomatoes

1½ cups tomato sauce

1½ cups shredded American cheese

1. Bring a 2-quart pot of water to a rolling boil. Add the pasta and cook according to package directions.

2. Heat the oil in a 4-quart pot over medium heat. Add the beef and cook, stirring often to crumble, for about 4 minutes, or until no pink remains. Drain off any excess fat.

3. Add the onions, celery, bell pepper, garlic, chili powder, cumin, and tamari to the pot and stir well. Sauté for about 7 minutes, or until the vegetables begin to soften and the onion is translucent.

4. Add the beans, tomatoes, and tomato sauce, and continue to cook, stirring occasionally, for 5 to 10 minutes, or until the chili is heated through.

5. Drain the cooked pasta, add it to the chili, and stir to mix.

6. Ladle the hot chili into bowls, top with shredded cheese, and serve.

MEATLESS CHOICE

- Replace the ground beef with 2 cups chopped or ground seitan. (It is not necessary to cook this. Simply add it to the pot along with the beans and tomatoes in Step 4.)
- Or replace the ground beef with 2 cups rehydrated TVP (1¾ cups dry TVP mixed with 1½ cups hot water and 2 teaspoons vegetarian beef bouillon). Like the seitan, simply add this ingredient in Step 4.

VEGAN CHOICE

- Use American soy cheese instead of regular American cheese.

Beef Stroganoff

Partially freezing the uncooked beef for this recipe will make it easier to slice. And meat that is thinly sliced usually assures tenderness. So, if possible, wrap the meat in plastic wrap and allow it to sit in the freezer for about thirty minutes before cutting.

1. Heat the oil in a 12-inch skillet over medium heat. Add the beef and garlic, and cook while stirring for 4 to 5 minutes, or until the meat is seared.

2. Add the onions and mushrooms, and continue cooking for another 3 minutes. Then stir in the milk, mustard, and tamari, and bring to a low boil.

3. Mix the cornstarch and water together, then add it to the skillet, stirring constantly until the sauce thickens.

4. Add the wine, and continue to cook another 10 minutes, then stir in the sour cream and simmer.

5. Spoon over pasta, noodles, rice, or mashed potatoes. Garnish with chopped parsley.

MEATLESS CHOICE

- Replace the beef with 2 cups thinly sliced seitan. (As this is already cooked, simply add it to the skillet in Step 2.)

VEGAN CHOICE

- Use soy milk instead of whole milk.
- Replace the sour cream with a soy-based variety, such as Soy Cashew Sour Cream (page 73).

Yield: 4 servings

1 tablespoon canola oil

2 cups very thinly sliced beef tenderloin or flank steak

1 1/2 teapoons minced fresh garlic

1 1/2 cups diced onions

1 1/2 cups sliced button mushrooms

1 cup whole milk

1 teaspoon Dijon mustard

3 tablespoons tamari or other soy sauce

3 tablespoons cornstarch or arrowroot

3 tablespoons water

3/4 cup sherry wine

3/4 cup sour cream

1/4 cup chopped fresh parsley for garnish

Beef Pepper Steak Pasta

There are many different ways to make pepper steak.
This version includes a wide range of flavorful
vegetables and herbs, and is served over pasta.

Yield: 4 servings

8 ounces angel hair pasta

2 tablespoons sesame oil

1 pound thinly sliced flank steak

2 cups diced onions

2 cups sliced mushrooms

1 cup diced red bell pepper

1 cup diced green bell pepper

2 teaspoons minced fresh garlic

1 teaspoon chopped fresh basil

1 teaspoon sea salt

2 cups French Brown Sauce
(page 80),
or other brown sauce variety

2 tablespoons tomato paste

1. Bring a 3- or 4-quart pot of water to a rolling boil. Add the pasta and cook according to package directions.

2. Heat the oil in a 12-inch skillet over medium heat. Add the beef, onions, mushrooms, bell peppers, garlic, basil, and salt, and sauté for 5 minutes, or until the beef is browned and the vegetables are beginning to soften.

3. Add the sauce and tomato paste to the skillet, stir the ingredients well, and simmer for 7 to 10 minutes.

4. Spoon the hot pepper steak over the cooked pasta and enjoy.

MEATLESS CHOICE

- Replace the beef with 3 cups chopped or thinly sliced seitan. (It is not necessary to cook this. Simply add it to the pot along with the sauce in Step 3.)

- If using French Brown Sauce, be sure it has been prepared with vegetarian beef bouillon.

Beef Schnitzel

Pounding the cutlets thinly will help ensure their tenderness.
This dish is perfect when accompanied by
creamy mashed potatoes.

1. Place the flour in a shallow plate and the bread crumbs in another. In a medium-sized bowl, beat together the eggs and water. Set aside.

2. Dredge the cutlets in flour, dip them in the egg mixture, then coat them with bread crumbs.

3. Heat 1 tablespoon of the oil in a 12-inch skillet over medium heat. Add the cutlets and brown lightly for 3 to 5 minutes on each side, or until the meat is cooked to the desired doneness. Transfer the cutlets to an ovenproof platter, and place in a warm oven until ready to serve.

4. Heat the remaining oil in the skillet over medium heat. Add the onions, carrots, garlic, caraway seeds, and salt, and sauté for 4 to 5 minutes, or until the onions begin to soften.

5. Add the cabbage and potatoes to the skillet, and continue to sauté for another 10 minutes. Stir in the wine, and cook covered for about 10 minutes, or until the cabbage and potatoes are soft. Add the liquid smoke and stir well.

6. Place the cutlets on a bed of cabbage and serve hot.

Yield: 8 servings

½ cup unbleached white flour

1 cup whole wheat bread crumbs

2 eggs

2 tablespoons water

8 thinly sliced beef cutlets
(about 6 ounces each)

3 tablespoons canola oil

2 cups sliced onions

1 cup coarsely grated carrots

1½ tablespoons minced fresh garlic

1½ teaspoons ground
caraway seeds

1½ teaspoons sea salt

6 cups shredded green cabbage

½ cup coarsely grated
new potatoes

1½ cups white wine

¾ teaspoon liquid smoke

MEATLESS CHOICE

- Replace the beef with thin slices of seitan, tempeh, or extra-firm tofu. You can also prepare the mixture for Tofu Pâté (page 141) and form it into patties. Dip the slices or patties in a bowl of water, then coat them with flour. Dip in water once more, coat with bread crumbs, and brown as instructed above.

VEGAN CHOICE

- Instead of beaten egg, use water.

Peasant Mostaccioli

Mostaccioli is a tube-shaped penne pasta, about 2 inches long. When I was in the Franciscan Order, this dish was a common one at the monastery–probably because it was both economical and easy to prepare. For a truly special variation, try this pasta with Walnut Pesto (page 71) instead of tomato sauce.

1. Bring a 4-quart pot of water to a rolling boil. Add the pasta, and cook according to package directions.

2. While the water is heating up, heat the oil in a 12-inch skillet over medium heat. Add the ground beef and cook, stirring often to crumble, for about 4 minutes, or until no pink remains. Drain off any excess fat.

3. Add the onions, carrots, garlic, and salt, and sauté for 5 minutes, or until the onions begin to soften. Add the mushrooms, basil, and sauce. Mix well, and continue to cook for 20 to 30 minutes.

4. Drain the cooked mostaccioli, return it to the pot, and add the sauce. Using a wooden spoon, stir the sauce and pasta together.

5. Spoon into dishes and serve hot.

MEATLESS CHOICE

- Replace the ground beef with 2 cups ground seitan. As the seitan doesn't have to be cooked, simply sauté it along with the onions and carrots.

VEGAN CHOICE

- Use soy Parmesan cheese instead of the regular variety.

Barbecued Pork

Although this tangy dish is made with pork,
it works just as well with chicken and beef.

1. Place the onions in a 12-inch skillet set over medium heat, and dry sauté them for 5 to 7 minutes, or until they begin to brown.

2. Add the oil and pork slices to the skillet. Cook, while stirring, for 5 to 7 minutes, or until the pork is no longer pink.

3. Add the barbecue sauce, molasses, and mustard to the skillet. Continue to cook for about 5 minutes.

4. Accompany with cornbread, or serve over polenta or rice.

Yield: 4 servings

2 cups diced onions

1 tablespoon sesame or canola oil

1 pound thinly sliced pork tenderloin

1 cup barbecue sauce

2 tablespoons molasses

4 teaspoons yellow prepared mustard

MEATLESS CHOICE

• Replace the pork with thinly sliced seitan. (It is not necessary to cook this. Simply add it to the skillet along with the sauce in Step 3.)

8

Inviting Vegetarian Fare

The vegetarian movement continues to gain in popularity. Whether for reasons of health, ethics, or just taste, this interest has resulted in delectable and creative vegetarian cuisine. No longer just for faddists, meatless meals provide an exciting change of pace from the traditional "meat and potato" meal.

This chapter begins by offering some vegetarian basics, such as the Tofu Pâté, and then goes on to present a dazzling array of meatless dishes. In the mood for a savory meat-like entrée? The Vegetarian Salisbury Steak is a great choice. If you're a pasta lover (and who isn't?), you will enjoy the unusual blend of ingredients in the Open-Face Black Olive Ravioli. Still other four-star entrées include satisfying French Onion Potato Quiche, mouthwatering Hazelnut-Crusted Stuffed Portabellas, and hot and hearty Quinoa Black Bean Stew. Don't miss these inviting selections.

If you have always preferred a vegetarian style of eating, or are simply interested in exploring vegetarian fare, you'll enjoy the collection of dishes on the following pages.

Sea Vegetable Tofu

These seafood-flavored rolls are excellent when topped with Roasted
Bell Pepper Sauce (page 85) or Lemon Olive Blanc (page 78).
They can also be cut into smaller pieces and used as an
alternative to shrimp, scallops, and many other fish varieties.

1. Preheat the oven to 350°F. Place the tofu mixture in a medium-sized bowl and set aside.

2. Heat 1 tablespoon of the oil in a 10-inch skillet over medium heat. Add the onions, carrots, garlic, lemon zest, and salt, and sauté for about 5 minutes, or until the vegetables begin to soften. Add the wakame, then transfer the mixture to the bowl with the tofu. Mix well.

3. If using dried egg roll wrappers, place them—two at a time—on a large dinner plate that is covered with water, and let them sit for about 1 minute, or until they are soft.

4. Place one of the softened wrappers on a clean work surface. Overlap the second wrapper over the bottom third of the first wrapper, and spoon 1/2 cup (8 tablespoons) of the mixture across the bottom. Tightly roll up (the ends will be open). Repeat with the remaining mixture and wrappers.

5. Heat the remaining tablespoon of oil in the skillet over medium heat. Place the rolls seal side down in the hot pan, and cook for 2 to 3 minutes, or until the bottoms are lightly brown. Using a spatula, carefully turn the rolls over and cook another 1 to 2 minutes.

6. Transfer the rolls seal side down to a lightly oiled baking sheet or casserole dish, and bake for 10 to 15 minutes. Serve hot.

Yield: 5 rolls

1 1/2 cups Tofu Pâté (page 141), or a smooth blend of 1 1/2 cups (12 ounces) extra-firm tofu, 4 teaspoons arrowroot, 2 teaspoons sesame oil, and 1/2 teaspoon agar powder

2 tablespoons canola oil

1 cup finely diced onions

1 cup shredded carrots

1 tablespoon chopped garlic

1 tablespoon lemon zest

1/2 teaspoon salt

1 tablespoon dry chopped wakame sea vegetable

10 egg roll wrappers (6-inch squares)*

1 tablespoon canola oil

* These wrappers come either in dried sheets, which need to be soaked and softened before using, or in convenient ready-to-use squares, which are found in the refrigerator section of most supermarkets.

VEGAN CHOICE

- Substitute spring roll wrappers for the egg roll wrappers.

Pâté Français

This pâté is formed into a roll and served in slices. I find it particularly good as an accompaniment to a fresh green salad.

Yield: 2 rolls
(about 10 inches long
and 3 inches in diameter)

2 cups dried navy beans, or 4 cups
canned variety, rinsed and drained

¼ teaspoon sea salt

1¼ cups walnut halves

½ cup black sesame seeds
(optional)

2 cups Tofu Pâté (page 141),
or a smooth blend of 2 cups
(1 pound) extra-firm tofu,
1½ tablespoons arrowroot,
1 teaspoon sesame oil, and
1 teaspoon agar powder

¼ cup minced fresh parsley

SEASONING BLEND

3 teaspoons paprika

2 teaspoons sea salt

1 teaspoon nutmeg

1 teaspoon ground ginger

1 teaspoon dry basil

1 teaspoon whole dry thyme

1 teaspoon dry marjoram

1 teaspoon ground allspice

1 teaspoon garlic powder

½ teaspoon black pepper

¼ teaspoon white pepper

1. Place the dried beans along with 6 cups of water in a 4-quart pot over high heat, and bring to a boil. Reduce the heat to low, and cook, covered, for about 30 minutes. Add the salt, and continue cooking for another 20 minutes, or until the beans are cooked, but firm.

2. Roast the walnuts and finely chop. (See roasting instructions on page 52.)

3. In a small mixing bowl, combine the seasoning blend ingredients and set aside. Place the sesame seeds (if using) in a shallow dish and set aside.

4. Place the tofu mixture in a large mixing bowl, add the seasoning blend and parsley, and mix until well blended. Stir in the navy beans and walnuts.

5. Lightly sprinkle some water on a clean counter and lay two sheets of plastic wrap on top (the water will prevent the wrap from moving). Spoon half of the tofu mixture across the bottom of each sheet in a 10-inch long mound. Tightly roll the mixture in the plastic and seal the ends. If using the sesame seeds, once the rolls are formed, unwrap them and roll in the seeds to coat. Rewrap the rolls in fresh sheets of plastic, seal well, then wrap them in a second piece of plastic. Finally, seal each roll in a sheet of aluminum foil.

6. Place the rolls on a steamer that is set over boiling water for about 30 minutes.

7. Transfer the steamed rolls to a platter, and refrigerate for 1 hour, or until cool.

8. To serve, remove the aluminum foil, and cut slices from the roll through the plastic wrap. Remove the wrap from the individual slices before serving.

Mushroom Pasta

A variety of mushrooms and flavorful herbs come together
to create this culinary masterpiece.

1. Bring a 4-quart pot of water to a rolling boil. Add the pasta, and cook according to package directions.

2. While the water is heating up, heat the oil in a 12-inch sauté pan over medium heat. Add the mushrooms, garlic, basil, and fennel, and sauté for about 7 minutes.

3. Add the Béchamel Sauce, cream, and wine to the pan. Stir well, and bring the ingredients to a boil. Reduce the heat to medium-low, and simmer for 7 to 10 minutes, or until the mixture has a creamy consistency.

4. Place equal amounts of pasta on two dinner plates, and top with sauce. Garnish with sundried tomatoes.

VEGAN CHOICE

- Replace the Béchamel Sauce with vegan variation (page 81).

- Instead of heavy cream, use Cashew Cream (page 76). You can also use a $\frac{1}{2}$ cup soy milk reduction. Do this by placing 1 cup of soy milk in a pan, and cooking it over medium heat until it is reduced to $\frac{1}{2}$ cup.

- Use soy Parmesan cheese instead of the regular variety.

Yield: 2 servings

8 ounces spaghetti, fettuccine, or angel hair pasta

2 tablespoons extra-virgin olive oil, or Basil Oil (page 68)

2 cups Portabella mushroom slices ($\frac{1}{4}$-inch-thick)

2 cups thickly sliced button mushrooms

1 tablespoon minced fresh garlic

1 $\frac{1}{2}$ teaspoons dry basil

1 teaspoon fennel powder

1 cup Béchamel Sauce (page 81), or commercial variety

$\frac{1}{2}$ cup heavy cream

$\frac{1}{4}$ cup white wine

$\frac{1}{4}$ cup chopped sundried tomatoes for garnish

Parmesan cheese for garnish

Open-Face Black Olive Ravioli

In this modern interpretation of a traditional food, lasagna noodles are cut in half and filled with a splendid combination of sweet dates and salty black olives. Although you can use any sauce to top these "ravioli," I recommend the Red Pepper Pesto. I also suggest serving them on a bed of braised fresh spinach.

Yield: 2 servings

3 wide lasagna noodles

¼ cup pine nuts

½ cup whole pitted
Kalamata olives

½ cup whole pitted dates

6 tablespoons Red Pepper
Pesto (page 70),
or sauce of choice

Parmesan cheese for garnish

1. Bring a 4-quart pot of water to a rolling boil. Add the lasagna noodles, and cook according to package directions.

2. While the water is heating up, roast the pine nuts according to the instructions on page 52. Then place them along with the olives and dates in a food processor, and process for 1 to 2 minutes, or until finely chopped into a paste.

3. Drain the cooked lasagna noodles, and blot any excess water with a paper towel. Cut the noodles in half crosswise. Place 2 tablespoons of the filling mixture on the center of each, then fold the top half of the noodle over the bottom half. Fold the noodle off center to expose a little of the dark filling.

4. Carefully place the "ravioli" on a lightly oiled steamer that is set over boiling water, and heat for 1 or 2 minutes. (You can also heat them in a lightly oiled sauté pan over medium heat.)

5. Top with sauce and serve with a sprinkling of Parmesan cheese. Try them over a bed of braised fresh spinach.

VEGAN CHOICE

• Use soy Parmesan cheese instead of the regular variety.

Tofu Pâté

I use this basic tofu pâté in many recipes—both vegetarian and nonvegetarian. It is so easy to make that I always have some on hand. Steaming the tofu allows this pâté to keep in the refrigerator for about a week. Without steaming, it will last three to four days.

1. Cut the tofu into four pieces and place on a steamer rack set over boiling water. Cover and steam for about 15 minutes.

2. Immediately transfer the tofu to a food processor along with the remaining ingredients. Process until smooth.

3. Place the tofu mixture in a container and refrigerate until ready to use.

Yield: About 4 cups

2 pounds extra-firm tofu

3 tablespoons arrowroot

2 tablespoons sesame or canola oil

1 tablespoon nutritional yeast (optional)

2 teaspoons agar powder, or 4 teaspoons flakes

1/2 teaspoon sea salt

WHEN COOKING PASTA

Vegetarians and nonvegetarians alike have long had a love affair with pasta. Not only is pasta inexpensive and nutritious, but it goes with almost any topping or sauce. When cooking pasta, keep the following general guidelines in mind:

☐ Two cups of uncooked pasta become about four cups when cooked.

☐ Always bring the water to a rolling boil before adding the uncooked pasta.

☐ Adding a little salt to the cooking water helps pasta hold its shape while adding a little flavor.

☐ Use a wooden spoon to stir the pasta. As the pasta softens, a metal spoon is likely to cut it.

☐ To prevent the pasta from sticking, stir it as soon as it is added to the boiling water. Then stir it every minute for the first five or six minutes.

☐ Be careful not to overcook pasta, which will cause it to become mushy. Properly cooked pasta should be firm to the bite, but not hard.

☐ Drain and serve cooked pasta immediately, or rinse it in cold water to stop the cooking process.

☐ If storing cooked pasta (to which sauce has not been added), toss it with a little oil to prevent it from sticking together. To reheat, simply submerge it in or run it under hot water.

Greek Quiche

*This is one of those dishes that is delicious
with or without cheese and eggs.*

Yield: 10-inch quiche

¹/₂ recipe Basic Pie Crust
(page 174), or commercial
single-crust pie shell

I egg

2 tablespoons arrowroot

I ¹/₂ teaspoons sea salt

2 pounds extra-firm tofu, pressed
to remove any excess water

³/₄ cup crumbled goat cheese

2 tablespoons extra-virgin olive oil

3 cups diced onions

¹/₂ cup finely diced red bell peppers

2 tablespoons chopped fresh basil

I tablespoon minced fresh garlic

I teaspoon chopped fresh oregano

4 cups chopped fresh spinach

¹/₂ cup chopped Kalamata olives

2 tablespoons chopped
fresh parsley

Chopped fresh parsley
for garnish

1. Preheat the oven to 375°F. Roll out the dough into an 11-inch circle, and press it into the bottom of a 10-inch pie plate. Roll up and crimp the edge. Set aside.

2. In a food processor, place the egg, arrowroot, salt, and half the tofu. Process to form a paste. Using your hands, crumble the remaining tofu and goat cheese together, and set aside.

3. Heat the oil in a 12-inch sauté pan over medium heat. Add the onions, bell peppers, basil, garlic, and oregano, and sauté for about 5 minutes, or until the onions are soft and transparent.

4. To the pan, add the crumbled tofu and spinach, and sauté with the other ingredients for about 5 minutes, or until the spinach wilts. Remove from the heat, and stir in the tofu paste, olives, and parsley. Mix well.

5. Pour the filling into the pie shell and bake 30 minutes, or until a knife inserted into the center of the pie comes out clean.

6. Allow the quiche to sit for 5 to 10 minutes before cutting and serving. Garnish with parsley and serve either hot or cold.

VEGAN CHOICE

- Simply eliminate the egg and goat cheese.

MEATEATER'S CHOICE

- Add 1 cup cooked ground lamb to the filling mixture. Sauté it with the other ingredients during Step 4.

French Onion Potato Quiche

If you enjoy the flavor combination of onions and potatoes, you'll love this quiche.

Yield: 10-inch quiche

½ recipe Basic Pie Crust (page 174), or commercial single-crust pie shell

2 tablespoons sesame or canola oil

8 cups thinly sliced onions (about 3 large)

I cup coarsely grated potatoes

1½ teaspoons sea salt

¼ teaspoon ground black pepper

⅛ teaspoon ground nutmeg

I cup whole milk

3 eggs

1. Preheat the oven to 375°F. Roll out the dough into an 11-inch circle, and press it into the bottom of a 10-inch pie plate. Roll up and crimp the edge. Set aside.

2. Heat the oil in a 12-inch sauté pan over medium heat. Add the onions, potatoes, salt, pepper, and nutmeg, and sauté for 5 minutes, or until the onions and potatoes are beginning to soften. Pour the mixture into the pie shell.

3. In a mixing bowl, whisk the milk and eggs together, then pour over the potatoes and onions. Gently shake the pie plate to ensure even distribution. Bake for 30 minutes, or until a knife inserted into the center of the pie comes out clean.

4. Allow the quiche to sit for 5 to 10 minutes before cutting and serving.

VEGAN CHOICE

- Replace the whole milk with ¾ cup soy milk.
- In place of the eggs, use a smooth blend of ½ cup extra-firm tofu and ¼ cup unbleached white flour. Incorporate the soy milk into this mixture, then add it to the potatoes and onions near the end of their sautéing time.

MEATEATER'S CHOICE

- Add ½ cup diced ham or Canadian bacon to the filling.

Portabella Mushroom Napoleon

I developed this recipe to serve on Christmas Day as a light holiday entrée.

1. Combine the marinade ingredients in a shallow baking dish. Add the mushroom caps, and turn to coat. Let sit in the marinade for 15 to 20 minutes at room temperature.

2. While the mushrooms are marinating, heat 1 tablespoon of the oil in a 12-inch skillet over medium heat. Add the egg roll skins, and lightly brown about 20 to 30 seconds on each side. Transfer the skins to a plate that is lined with paper towels to absorb any excess oil.

3. Heat the remaining oil in the skillet over medium heat. Add the marinated mushroom caps, and sauté them for 4 to 5 minutes on each side. Transfer to a plate and set aside.

4. Add the onions to the skillet and sauté, stirring occasionally, for 7 to 10 minutes, or until the onions begin to turn brown and caramelize. Add the basil and bell peppers, and continue to sauté for 4 to 5 minutes. Remove from the heat and set aside.

5. Thinly slice the mushroom caps on a 45-degree angle to get 24 slices.

6. In a medium saucepan, warm the sauce.

7. To assemble the Napoleons, place an egg roll skin on a plate, top with $^1/_2$ cup of onion mixture and 3 mushroom slices. Spoon $^1/_4$ cup of sauce over the mushrooms. Cover with another egg roll skin, and repeat the process, topping the stack with a third skin.

VEGAN CHOICE

• Replace the egg roll skins with phyllo pastry. (Instructions for making phyllo squares are given in the Colorado Bean Stack recipe on page 146.)

MEATEATER'S CHOICE

- Replace the Portabella mushrooms with thinly sliced grilled lamb, chicken, or beef. Roasted duck is another good choice for this recipe. I recommend using Bigarade Sauce (page 81), with the duck version, and French Brown Sauce (page 80) with the other meats.

Winter Vegetable Stew

Once you have eaten this stew, which is rich in both flavor and texture, you will never forget it. Enjoy it with Grandma's Favorite Biscuits (page 35).

Yield: 8 servings

2 tablespoons canola or sesame oil

2 cups diced Spanish onions

2 tablespoons minced fresh garlic

1 tablespoon dry thyme

1 1/2 cups diced rutabaga

1 1/2 cups carrots, cut into 1/4-inch-thick rounds

1 1/2 cups parsnips, cut into 1/4-inch-thick rounds

1 1/2 cups diced turnips

1 can (15 ounces) chickpeas

3 cups water

3 tablespoons dark miso

6 tablespoons water

2 tablespoons arrowroot

4 tablespoons water

1. Heat the oil in a 3-quart saucepan over medium heat. Add the onions, garlic, and thyme, and stir well. Next add the rutabaga, carrots, parsnips, and turnips, and sauté for about 10 minutes.

2. Add the beans and water, and simmer for about 10 more minutes or until the vegetables are cooked.

3. Dissolve the miso in 5 or 6 tablespoons of water, and add it to the stew. Dissolve arrowroot in 3 or 4 tablespoons of water, and stir it into the stew. While stirring, cook the stew another 5 minutes, or until it thickens.

4. Spoon the piping hot stew over mashed potatoes, rice, or pasta.

MEATEATER'S CHOICE

- Replace the beans with 2 cups diced cooked lamb, beef, or chicken.
- If using chicken, substitute white miso for the dark.
- Use 2 cups chicken broth instead of water.

Colorado Bean Stack

Not only is this dish delicious, it is beautiful to look at and versatile, too. Feel free to use chickpeas or black beans in place of the pinto beans, or replace the Onion-Garlic Cream Sauce with fresh salsa. Sometimes I omit the phyllo altogether and serve the bean mixture over rice.

Yield: 6 servings

¼ cup pine nuts

4 full sheets phyllo pastry dough

2 tablespoons sesame oil

2 cups sliced Spanish onions

1½ cups carrots, cut into ¼-inch-thick rounds

1 cup diced red bell peppers

1 cup frozen whole kernel corn

1 tablespoon minced fresh garlic

2 teaspoons dry whole savory

1 teaspoon dry thyme

¾ teaspoon sea salt

1 can (15 ounces) pinto beans

2 cups Onion-Garlic Cream Sauce (page 79)

1. Roast the pine nuts according to the instructions on page 52. Remove the roasted nuts from the baking sheet, and set aside to cool.

2. Lay a sheet of phyllo on an oiled baking sheet. Lightly brush the top with oil, and cover with another phyllo sheet. Repeat with the process with all four sheets. Cut the phyllo into 12 pieces (3-x-4-inches each), and bake for about 5 minutes, or until light brown. Immediately remove from oven, and transfer the phyllo squares to paper towels. (Leaving them on the hot baking sheet will cause them to burn.)

3. Heat the oil in a 12-inch sauté pan over medium heat. Add the onions, carrots, bell peppers, corn, garlic, savory, thyme, and salt. Cover and sauté, stirring occasionally, for 10 minutes, or until the vegetables are soft.

4. Add the beans, pine nuts, and sauce to the pan, and stir well. Simmer on low heat for 5 minutes, or until thoroughly heated.

5. To serve, spoon ½ cup of the bean mixture onto a plate, and top with a phyllo square. Repeat the process, topping the stack with a third square of phyllo. Serve immediately while the filling is hot and the pastry is crisp.

VEGAN CHOICE

- Prepare the Onion-Garlic Cream Sauce with soy milk instead of cream.

MEATEATER'S CHOICE

- Replace half of the beans with 1¼ pounds sautéed chicken breast strips.
- Or simply add some sautéed chicken breast strips to the mixture without eliminating any beans.

Quinoa
Black Bean Stew

Quinoa is an ancient millet-like grain. It is added to this stew along with loads of fresh vegetables, hearty black beans, and lots of flavorful herbs and spices. Because this dish keeps in the refrigerator for about a week, I always make a big pot and enjoy it for several days.

Yield: 9 servings

2 tablespoons sesame oil

3 cups diced onions

2 cups diced red potatoes

2 cups thinly sliced leeks

2 cups thinly sliced celery

1½ cups carrots, cut into ¼-inch-thick rounds

1 cup diced red bell peppers

2 tablespoons chopped fresh garlic

4 cups coarsely chopped green cabbage

3 cups diced butternut squash

10 cups water

1 cup quinoa, rinsed and drained

2 tablespoons herbamare, or salt to taste

2 teaspoons ground cumin

1 can (15 ounces) black beans, rinsed and drained

1 cup chopped fresh parsley

1 cup chopped fresh cilantro

1. Heat the oil in an 8-quart stockpot over medium heat. Add the onions, potatoes, leeks, celery, carrots, bell peppers, and garlic. Sauté for about 10 minutes, or until the vegetables begin to soften.

2. Add the cabbage, squash, water, quinoa, herbamare, and cumin, and cook for 10 minutes, or until the squash is soft.

3. Add the beans to the pot along with the parsley and cilantro, and stir well. Heat thoroughly.

4. Ladle the hot stew into bowls and enjoy.

MEATEATER'S CHOICE

- Add 2 pounds of cubed cooked chicken to the stew 5 minutes before serving.

Hazelnut-Crusted Stuffed Portabellas

*This superbly decked out Portabella mushroom
won a silver medal in the
International Culinary Olympics.*

Yield: 3 servings

3 Portabella mushroom caps
(about 6-inches each)

2 tablespoons canola
or extra-virgin olive oil

I cup finely diced or grated carrots

I pound extra-firm tofu

1/2 cup crumbled feta cheese

4 1/2 teaspoons arrowroot

I tablespoon sesame oil

I teaspoon agar powder

1/4 teaspoon sea salt

1/4 teaspoon liquid smoke, optional

1/4 cup chopped fresh parsley

1/2 cup unbleached white flour

1/2 cup finely ground hazelnuts

1. Preheat the oven to 350°F. Using a teaspoon, carefully remove the gills from the underside of each mushroom. Lightly salt the bottoms and set aside.

2. Heat 1 tablespoon of the oil in 12-inch sauté pan over medium heat. Place the mushrooms in the pan salted side down. Sauté for 5 minutes, gently pressing the mushrooms with a spatula to extract moisture. Remove from pan and press with paper towels to extract additional moisture.

3. In the same pan, add another tablespoon of oil and the carrots. Sauté for about 3 minutes, and then remove from the heat.

4. Place the tofu, feta cheese, arrowroot, sesame oil, agar powder, sea salt, and liquid smoke (if using) in a food processor, and process until smooth. Transfer the mixture to a large mixing bowl, along with the sautéed carrots and chopped parsley. Mix well and set aside.

5. Flour the inside of the mushroom caps, then fill each with the tofu-carrot mixture. Coat both sides of the mushrooms with flour. Brush water on the unfilled side of each cap, coat with flour, then sprinkle with more water so the flour is wet and pasty. Press this side of each cap into the hazelnut meal, and shake gently to remove any excess meal.

6. Heat the remaining oil in the sauté pan over medium heat. Add the caps nut-side up, and cook for 3 minutes, or until the filled bottoms are lightly brown. Transfer to a baking sheet, and bake for 10 to 15 minutes, or until the caps are heated through, and the nuts are lightly brown.

7. Remove from the oven, and cool the mushrooms for 5 minutes, or until they are cool enough to handle, but still warm. Cut the mushrooms on a 45-degree angle into ¹/₂-inch-thick slices. Serve with your favorite brown sauce. French Brown Sauce (page 80) and Forager's Sauce (page 90) are recommended choices.

VEGAN CHOICE

• Eliminate the feta cheese.

• If using French Brown Sauce, be sure it is made with vegetarian beef bouillon.

Caribbean Black Beans

Cornbread is an excellent accompaniment to this dish.
Try the Carrot Cornbread on page 34.

Yield: 4 servings

2 cups diced onions

1 tablespoon sesame oil

³/₄ cup favorite barbecue sauce

1 can (15-ounces) black beans, drained

2 cups diced fresh mangoes

¹/₄ teaspoon sea salt

¹/₄ teaspoon ground coriander

¹/₄ cup coconut milk

1. In a 12-inch skillet over medium heat, add the onions and dry sauté them for 7 to 10 minutes, or until they are lightly browned.

2. Add the sesame oil, barbecue sauce, black beans, and mangoes. Stir to mix well, then add the salt, coriander, and coconut milk. Heat thoroughly.

3. Serve hot over a bed of rice. The Coconut Rice on page 167 is recommended.

MEATEATER'S CHOICE

• Eliminate 8 ounces (1 cup) of beans, and replace it with cubes of cooked pork or ham. Seafood lovers can replace the beans with 8 ounces of raw shrimp or scallops. All of these substitutions should be added during the last 10 to 15 minutes of cooking time.

Pistachio-Crusted Tofu with Pasta

Ground pistachio nuts add an interesting dimension to the tofu in this dish, which I created for my friends Peter and Nancy.

Yield: 4 servings

8 ounces spaghetti, fettuccine, or angel hair pasta

1 pound block extra-firm tofu, rinsed and drained

½ cup unbleached white flour

½ teaspoon ground fennel

¼ teaspoon sea salt

1 cup ground pistachios

1 tablespoon extra-virgin olive oil

12 tablespoons (¾ cup) Balsamic Demi-Glace (page 83)

Chopped tomatoes for garnish

Chopped parsley for garnish

1. Bring a 4-quart pot of water to a rolling boil. Add the pasta, and cook according to package directions.

2. While the water for the pasta is heating up, slice the block of tofu into quarters, and then cut each quarter in half for a total of 8 equal pieces. Set aside.

3. In a mixing bowl, combine the flour, fennel, and salt. Dredge the tofu in the flour mixture to coat well.

4. Lightly brush each piece of floured tofu with water, making sure all sides are moist. Cover the tofu with the ground pistachios, and press to coat well. Set aside.

5. Heat the oil in a 12-inch skillet over medium-low heat. Add the tofu and cook about 30 to 60 seconds on each side, or until lightly browned.

6. To serve, mound equal amounts of pasta in the center of four dinner plates, and drizzle 2 tablespoons of the demi-glace over each. Lean two pieces of tofu on either side of each mound. Drizzle with more demi-glace, and garnish with tomatoes and parsley.

MEATEATER'S CHOICE

- Instead of tofu, use 4 strips of boneless chicken breast (about 4 ounces each). Butterfly-cut the breasts to make them thin. After covering the chicken pieces with nuts, bake them in a 350°F oven for about 10 minutes, or until cooked through. (It is important that the chicken is no more than ½ inch thick, or the nuts may burn before the meat is cooked.)

Zucchini Pancakes

*While these pancakes are a great breakfast item,
I often serve them for dinner as a light entrée.*

1. Place all of the ingredients except the oil in a large mixing bowl. Stir well to combine.

2. Heat the oil on a griddle over medium-low heat. Spoon ½-cup portions of the mixture onto the hot griddle, and smooth them into 3- to 4-inch pancakes. Cook for 3 to 5 minutes, or until the bottoms of the pancakes are lightly brown. Using a spatula, turn the pancakes over and cook for another 3 to 4 minutes.

3. Serve the pancakes hot.

VEGAN CHOICE

- Replace the eggs with 1 cup Tofu Pâté (page 141), or a smooth blend of 1 cup (8 ounces) extra-firm tofu, 2¼ teaspoons arrowroot, 1½ teaspoons sesame oil, and ½ teaspoon agar powder.

- Use soy Parmesan cheese instead of the regular variety.

Yield: 6 pancakes

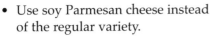

2 cups coarsely grated zucchini

1½ cups diced onions

1 cup coarsely grated carrots

¼ cup unbleached white flour

3 beaten eggs

1 tablespoon vegetable base

2 tablespoons Parmesan cheese

1 teaspoon sea salt

2 tablespoons canola oil

Sea Vegetable Corn Cakes

This vegan option rivals the original recipe on page 107.
It won a gold medal in the American Sea Vegetable
Study at the 1996 International Culinary Olympics.
You will know why when you treat yourself to it.

Yield: 16 cakes
(about 3-inches),
or 32 appetizer-sized cakes

1 cup finely diced onions

1 cup finely diced red bell pepper

1 cup finely diced green bell pepper

1 cup cooked whole kernel corn
(canned or frozen/thawed
varieties are fine)

2 tablespoons instant dry
wakame sea vegetable

1/2 teaspoon dry thyme

1 tablespoon plus 2 teaspoons
canola oil

1/4 cup Soy Mayonnaise (page 64),
or commercial variety

1 1/2 tablespoons Dijon mustard

1 1/2 teaspoons Worcestershire
Sauce

1/4 teaspoon Tabasco sauce

1 cup Tofu Pâté (page 141),
or a smooth blend of
1 cup (8 ounces) tofu,
2 1/4 teaspoons arrowroot,
1 1/2 teaspoons sesame oil,
and 1/2 teaspoon agar powder

1 tablespoon Old Bay seasoning

1/2 cup bread crumbs

1. In a 12-inch sauté pan over medium-low heat, add the onions, bell peppers, corn, wakame, and thyme, and dry sauté for 5 minutes, or until the vegetables have released their moisture and the wakame is rehydrated. Add 1 tablespoon of the oil and continue sautéing for 5 to 7 minutes, or until the vegetables are soft. Transfer the mixture to a baking sheet, and spread it out to cool. Blot any excess moisture with paper towels.

2. In a large mixing bowl, combine the mayonnaise, mustard, Worcestershire sauce, and Tabasco sauce. Add the sautéed vegetables and Tofu Pâté, and mix well.

3. In a separate mixing bowl, add the Old Bay seasoning to the bread crumbs, and combine well. Add the crumbs to the tofu mixture, and mix until well combined.

4. Form 1/4-cup portions of the mixture into 16 patties. To make 32 appetizer-sized cakes, use 2-tablespoon portions.

5. Heat the remaining 2 teaspoons of oil in the sauté pan over medium-low heat. When the oil is hot, add the patties. Cook for 3 to 5 minutes, or until the bottoms of the patties are brown. Using a spatula, carefully turn them over, and continue to cook another 3 minutes, or until browned on the second side.

6. Serve immediately.

Vegetarian Salisbury Steak

Using texturized vegetable protein (TVP) instead of ground beef results in a vegetarian Salisbury steak that rivals the original in taste. The meateater's version of this dish is found on page 127.

1. Preheat the oven to 350°F.

2. Heat 1 tablespoon of the oil in a 12-inch sauté pan over medium heat. Add the onions, mushrooms, garlic, basil, thyme, and salt. Sauté 5 to 7 minutes, or until onions are soft and transparent. Remove from the heat and set aside.

3. In a large mixing bowl, combine the flour, tamari, TVP, and Tofu Pâté. Add the sautéed vegetables, and mix by hand until well combined. Form the mixture into 6 oval-shaped patties.

4. Heat the remaining tablespoon of oil in the sauté pan over medium heat. Add the patties and brown the bottoms for 3 to 5 minutes. Using a spatula, turn the patties over, and brown the other side for another 3 minutes.

5. Transfer the cooked patties to a baking dish, and top with the sauce. Cover and bake for 15 to 20 minutes, or until the "steaks" are cooked. Serve hot with creamy mashed potatoes.

* For 12 ounces rehydrated TVP, mix ¾ cup dry TVP with 1½ cups hot water and 2 teaspoons vegetarian beef bouillon.

Yield: 6 servings

2 tablespoons canola or sesame oil

I cup finely diced onions

I cup finely diced mushrooms

I tablespoon minced fresh garlic

I teaspoon dry basil

I teaspoon dry thyme

I teaspoon sea salt

¼ cup unbleached white flour

2 tablespoons tamari
or other soy sauce

12 ounces rehydrated TVP*
(texturized vegetable protein),
or cooked bulghur

2 cups Tofu Pâté (page 141),
or a smooth blend of 2 cups
(I pound) extra-firm tofu,
4½ teaspoons arrowroot,
3 tablespoons sesame oil,
and I teaspoon agar powder

3 cups French Brown Sauce
(page 80),
or other brown sauce variety

VEGAN CHOICE

- If using French Brown Sauce, be sure it has been prepared with vegetarian beef bouillon.

9

Show-Stopping Side Dishes

Although a main dish should be the star of a meal, the side dish can play an all-important supporting role. With the right combination of ingredients, the simple side dish can be just as inspiring and tantalizing as your choice of entrée.

A wealth of outstanding vegetable recipes and a number of hearty grain dishes are offered in this chapter. You'll find fluffy rice and barley pilafs, as well as flavorful risottos. Tangy cranberries give Sweet Potato Pancakes a spark of flavor, while sage and garlic add an interesting twist to creamy Sage Mashed Potatoes. Hot and crisp Breaded Zucchini Rounds are a popular choice, as are the Fried Green Tomatoes with Peanut Sauce. Vegetables like Brussels sprouts, squash, eggplant, and field greens are featured in this chapter, as well as sea vegetables such as arame.

Selecting the right side dish will add to the full dining experience. Enjoy poring through the enticing creations offered on the pages that follow. Each and every one is a masterpiece.

Breaded Zucchini Rounds

Don't expect any leftovers when serving these tasty zucchini rounds.
When served hot and crisp, they're irresistible

1. In a medium mixing bowl, whisk together the eggs and water.

2. In a second bowl, combine the flour, bread crumbs, vegetable base, and salt. Mix well.

3. Dip the zucchini rounds in the egg mixture, then transfer them to the bowl with the bread crumb mixture. Coat the slices well, gently pressing the crumbs to cover both sides. Set aside.

4. Heat the oil in a 12-inch skillet over medium heat. Add the breaded zucchini, and sauté for about 2 minutes, or until the bottoms are brown. Using a fork, turn the slices over and cook another minute, or until the second sides are brown. Transfer to a paper towel-lined plate.

5. Serve while hot and crisp, with a sprinkling of Parmesan cheese.

VEGAN CHOICE

- For a vegan way to prepare these zucchini rounds, follow the method used for the Vegan-Style Breaded Yellow Squash on page 158.

Yield: 2 servings

2 eggs

2 tablespoons water

$1/4$ cup unbleached white flour

$1/4$ cup bread crumbs

2 tablespoons vegetable base powder

$1/2$ teaspoon sea salt

8 zucchini rounds ($1/2$ inch thick)

$1/4$ cup extra-virgin olive oil

Parmesan cheese, optional

Vegan-Style Breaded Yellow Squash

Crisp and tasty, these breaded squash rounds should be enjoyed as soon as they are cooked.

1. Fill a medium-sized mixing bowl with water. In a second mixing bowl, combine the white flour, vegetable broth powder, and gluten flour, and set aside. Place the bread crumbs in a shallow dish, and set aside.

2. Using tongs, dip each squash round quickly in and out of the water, and into the flour mixture. Let sit in the flour about 10 seconds, dip quickly back into the water, and then place in the bowl with the bread crumbs. Coat the slice well, gently pressing the crumbs to cover both sides. Set aside.

3. Heat the oil in a 12-inch skillet over medium heat. Add the breaded zucchini, and sauté for about 2 minutes, or until the bottoms are brown. Using a fork, turn the slices over and cook another minute, or until the second sides are brown. Transfer to a paper towel-lined plate.

4. Serve while hot and crisp, with a sprinkling of soy Parmesan cheese.

Quinoa Black Bean Stew (page 147)
[TOP LEFT]
Pistachio-Crusted Tofu (page 150)
with Balsamic Demi-Glace (page 83)
[TOP RIGHT]
Colorado Bean Stack (page 146)
[BOTTOM LEFT]

Fried Green Tomatoes with Peanut Sauce

*This fusion of ethnic dishes combines fried green tomatoes—
a specialty from the Southern United States—
with Asian-style peanut sauce.*

1. Cut the tomatoes into ¼-inch-thick slices, and discard the ends. Pat the slices with paper towels to absorb any excess moisture.

2. Place the eggs in a small bowl and whisk until frothy. Combine the corn flour, fennel powder, and salt in a mixing bowl and set aside.

3. Dip the tomato slices quickly into the egg, and then place them in the flour mixture. Coat the slices evenly.

4. Heat the oil in a 10-inch skillet over medium-low heat. When the oil is hot, add the tomatoes, and fry for about 1 minute, or until the bottoms are lightly brown. Carefully turn the slices and brown the remaining side. Transfer the cooked tomatoes to a paper towel-lined plate.

5. Heat the sauce in a small pan over medium-low heat.

6. Serve the tomatoes hot and crisp, and drizzled with sauce.

VEGAN CHOICE

- Omit the eggs, and add 2 tablespoons gluten flour to the corn flour mixture. When coating the tomato slices, first dip them in water, then coat them with the flour mixture. Quickly dip the slices back into the water, and coat once more with the flour mixture. Fry as instructed.

Yield: 4 servings

3 medium-sized green tomatoes

2 eggs

½ cup corn flour

½ teaspoon fennel powder

½ teaspoon sea salt

¼ cup peanut oil

½ cup Asian Peanut Sauce (page 85), or other commercial variety

Carrots and Leeks
with Sea Vegetables

The strong earthy flavor of the burdock complements the
milder-flavored carrots and leeks in this vegetable side dish.

Yield: 5 servings

$\frac{1}{2}$ cup dry arame

1$\frac{1}{4}$ cups plus 1 cup water

1 tablespoon plus 2 tablespoons
tamari or other soy sauce

1 tablespoon sesame oil

2 cups julienne-cut carrots

1 cup julienne-cut burdock

1$\frac{1}{2}$ teaspoons dry thyme

2 cups thinly sliced
fresh leeks

1. In a small saucepan, combine the arame, 1$\frac{1}{4}$ cups of the water, and 1 tablespoon of the tamari. Cover and place over medium-low heat for 10 to 15 minutes, or until the arame is hydrated and all of the water is absorbed. Set aside.

2. Heat the oil in a 12-inch sauté pan over medium heat. Add the carrots, burdock, arame, and thyme. Sauté for about 10 minutes.

3. Add the leeks, and the remaining water and tamari. Cook another 5 to 10 minutes, or until the vegetables are completely cooked. (If the water evaporates before the vegetables are cooked, add another $\frac{1}{4}$ cup of water and cook a little longer.)

4. Serve hot.

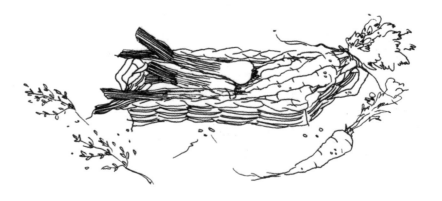

Sautéed Brussels Sprouts

Brussels sprouts are among my favorite vegetables. In this dish, they are sautéed with flavorful Canadian bacon and ground caraway seeds.

1. Heat the oil in a 12-inch sauté pan over medium heat. Add the Brussels sprouts, bell peppers, Canadian bacon, salt, and caraway seeds, and sauté for 3 to 5 minutes, stirring occasionally.

2. Add the water, cover, and cook another 5 minutes, or until the water has nearly evaporated. Serve immediately.

MEATLESS CHOICE

- Eliminate the Canadian bacon, or use a vegetarian-style Canadian bacon or ham instead.

Yield: 3 servings

1 tablespoon canola oil

1 ½ cups halved Brussels sprouts

1 ½ cups diced red bell peppers

¼ cup shredded Canadian bacon

½ teaspoon sea salt

¼ teaspoon ground caraway seeds

½ cup water

Sautéed Eggplant With Wine

This recipe will enliven most pasta dishes.

1. Heat the oil in a 12-inch sauté pan over medium heat. Add the eggplant, onions, garlic, and fennel, and sauté for 5 minutes, or until the vegetables begin to soften.

2. Add the broth, vinegar, wine, tomato paste, and salt. Let the eggplant simmer for 15 minutes. Serve hot.

MEATLESS CHOICE

- Replace the chicken broth with water or vegetarian chicken broth. (If using water, add an additional ½ teaspoon salt.)

Yield: 4 servings

3 tablespoons extra-virgin olive oil

6 cups diced eggplant (1-inch pieces)

1 ½ cups diced onions

2 tablespoons minced fresh garlic

1 teaspoon ground fennel

1 cup chicken broth

½ cup balsamic vinegar

½ cup red wine

¼ cup tomato paste

½ teaspoon sea salt

Tuscan Vegetables

Nancy and I often enjoy this side dish
of sautéed vegetables as a light dinner entrée.

1. Heat the oil in a 12-inch sauté pan over medium heat. Add all of the ingredients, and sauté for 5 to 7 minutes, or until the vegetables are cooked, but firm.

2. Serve immediately.

Moroccan Ratatouille

Harissa Sauce gives this ratatouille unique flavor.

Yield: 4 servings

2 tablespoons extra-virgin olive oil

2 cups large diced zucchini

2 cups large diced eggplant

I cup large diced Spanish onions

I cup large diced yellow squash

½ cup large diced red bell peppers

I teaspoon sea salt

1½ cups Harissa Sauce (page 77)

¼ cup chopped fresh parsley for garnish

1. Heat the oil in a deep 12-inch skillet over medium-high heat. Add the zucchini, eggplant, onions, squash, bell peppers, and salt, and sauté for 5 to 7 minutes, or until the vegetables are lightly browned.

2. Add the sauce, and cook another 7 to 10 minutes.

3. Sprinkle with parsley and serve immediately.

Risotto Pesto

Risotto is a rice dish in which hot liquid is added gradually to grains of Arborio rice as they cook. The result is a heavenly blend of slightly chewy rice that is enveloped in a wonderfully silky sauce.

1. Wash and rinse the rice.

2. Heat a 12-inch skillet over medium heat. Add the rice, and sauté, stirring often, for a minute to eliminate some of the water from the wet rice. Add the oil, then sauté for about 3 minutes, or until lightly brown.

3. Add the onions and garlic, and continue sautéing for 5 minutes, or until the onions begin to soften. Slowly stir 3 cups of the hot broth into the rice mixture, and simmer for 30 minutes. While stirring, slowly add the chicken bouillon and the remaining broth to the rice. Continue to simmer another 20 to 30 minutes, or until most of the broth is absorbed and the rice is cooked, yet firm. Add the pesto and stir well to combine.

4. Serve immediately.

Yield: 6 servings

1 ½ cups brown Arborio rice

2 tablespoons extra-virgin olive oil

2 cups finely chopped onion

1 tablespoon minced fresh garlic

4 cups hot chicken broth

3 tablespoons chicken bouillon

6 tablespoons Walnut Pesto (page 71)

VEGAN CHOICE

- Instead of chicken broth, use vegetable broth or water.
- Use vegetarian chicken base instead of chicken bouillon.

Sweet Potato Pancakes

The tangy sweetness of cranberries gives added spark to these crisp potato treats, which are my wife Nancy's favorite Sunday morning breakfast. She enjoys them with applesauce.

1. Place the sweet potatoes and 1 cup of the water in a 10-inch skillet over medium heat. Cover and steam for 10 minutes, or until the potatoes start to soften. Transfer the potatoes to a plate, and set aside.

2. In a large mixing bowl, combine the red potatoes with the salt and the remaining 2 cups of water. Let stand for 20 minutes, then rinse, drain, and press dry.

3. To the red potatoes, add the sweet potatoes, onions, parsley, flour, eggs, cranberries, and herbamare. Mix well.

4. Heat half of the oil in the skillet over medium-low heat. When the oil is hot, add ½- cup portions of the potato mixture to the skillet, and press to flatten. Cook for 3 to 5 minutes, or until the bottoms are brown. Turn the pancakes over and brown the other side.

5. Transfer the cooked pancakes to a paper towel-lined plate, and repeat Step 4 with the remaining potato mixture. Serve hot and crisp.

VEGAN CHOICE

- Eliminate the eggs, and add another ¼ cup of unbleached white flour to the potato mixture.

Braised Field Greens with Caramelized Onions

Field greens typically include tender vegetables like baby bok choy and chard, as well as spinach and kale. They are available during the summer months at most farmers' markets. Although this recipe is technically a side dish, I often enjoy it over mashed potatoes as a complete meal.

1. In a 12-inch sauté pan over medium heat, add the onions and eggplant. Dry sauté, stirring occasionally, for 7 to 10 minutes, or until light brown. Transfer to a mixing bowl, and set aside.

2. Heat the oil in the same sauté pan over medium heat. Add the bell peppers and salt, and sauté for 3 minutes, or until the peppers begin to soften.

3. Add the greens to the pan, and continue sautéing until they are wilted and cooked.

4. Add the eggplant mixture, and toss the ingredients together for 30 seconds, or until the vegetables are heated through.

5. Enjoy hot.

Yield: 5 servings

2 cups onion slices

2 cups diced eggplant

2 tablespoons extra-virgin olive oil

1 cup diced red bell peppers

1 teaspoon sea salt

4 cups field greens of choice

Sage Mashed Potatoes

This recipe complements most meat and poultry dishes as well as vegetarian foods, such as seitan. For potatoes that are light and fluffy, whip them as soon as they are cooked.

Yield: 6 servings

8 cups diced unpeeled potatoes

¼ cup butter

12 chopped fresh sage leaves, or 1½ teaspoons dry

2 teaspoons minced fresh garlic

1½ teaspoons sea salt

½ cup hot milk

1. In a 3-quart saucepan over medium heat, add the potatoes with enough water to cover. Bring to a boil, then reduce the heat and simmer the potatoes for 20 to 30 minutes, or until they are soft.

2. Drain the potatoes and transfer them to the bowl of an electric mixer, along with the butter, sage, garlic, and salt. Whip on medium speed for 2 to 3 minutes, or until soft and creamy. Reduce the mixer speed to low, and gradually add the milk. Mix another 30 seconds on high speed.

3. Transfer the mashed potatoes to a bowl and serve immediately.

VEGAN CHOICE

- Substitute canola oil for the butter.
- Instead of whole milk, use soy milk or water.

Three-Grain Pilaf

Try this easy-to-prepare pilaf as an accompaniment to Salmon Niçoise (page 108) or Beef Stroganoff (page 129).

1. In a medium-sized bowl, combine the barley, basmati rice, and Wehani rice. Rinse grains thoroughly and drain.

2. Transfer the grains to a 3-quart saucepan along with the broth and salt. Bring to a boil over medium heat. Reduce the heat to low, and simmer, covered, for approximately 35 to 45 minutes, or until the broth is absorbed and the rice is soft.

3. Serve immediately.

MEATLESS CHOICE

- Use vegetable broth or water instead of chicken or beef broth.

Yield: 6 servings

1/2 cup pearl barley

1/2 cup basmati rice

1/2 cup Wehani rice*, or wild rice

3 1/2 cups low-sodium chicken or beef broth

Pinch sea salt

A hybrid rice, Wehani is available in many specialty shops and health food stores.

Coconut Rice

Basmati is an aromatic long-grained rice that is native to India. I recommend this version with Caribbean Black Beans (page 149).

1. Place all of the ingredients in a 2-quart pot over medium heat. Mix well.

2. Bring the ingredients to a boil, then reduce the heat to medium-low. Cook for about 30 minutes, or until the liquid is absorbed and the rice is tender.

3. Fluff the rice with a fork, and serve immediately.

MEATLESS CHOICE

- Use vegetable broth or water instead of chicken stock.

Yield: 4 servings

2 cups basmati rice

1 cup coconut milk

1 cup chicken broth

1/2 cup finely diced onions

Pinch sea salt

Niçoise Couscous

Couscous—also known as Moroccan pasta—couldn't be simpler to make. To ensure the lightness of this dish, fluff the cooked couscous before adding the sauce.

Yield: 4 servings

1 tablespoon extra-virgin olive oil

1 cup couscous

$\frac{1}{4}$ teaspoon sea salt

1$\frac{1}{2}$ cups chicken broth

1 cup Sauce Niçoise (page 82)

3 tablespoons grated Parmesan cheese

1. Heat the oil in a 3-quart saucepan over medium heat. Add the couscous and cook, stirring constantly, for about 2 minutes. Add the salt, stir in the broth, and remove from the heat.

2. Cover and let sit for 15 minutes.

3. Fluff the cooked couscous with a fork, and then add the sauce and cheese. Stir to combine well.

4. Serve hot.

VEGAN CHOICE

- In place of the chicken broth, use water or vegetable broth.
- Prepare the Sauce Niçoise without the anchovies.
- Use soy Parmesan cheese instead of the regular variety.

10

Decadent Desserts

Ah, dessert. The meal's crowning glory. The right dessert can be as simple as a piece of nature-sweetened fruit or as intricate as a triple-layered cream-filled Napoleon.

This chapter presents a wide range of taste-tempting desserts, including pies, cakes, cookies, truffles, puddings, and sorbets. It also includes a delicious assortment of both toppings and sauces. Whatever you're craving, you'll find it here. In the mood for something simple? Nothing fills the bill better than a scoop of Cranberry Sorbet or a serving of Fresh Summer Fruit Salad. But when it's something sinfully rich you desire, perhaps a slice of Pineapple Mango Pie or Walnut Tart is a more satisfying choice. And when entertaining guests, do not pass up the opportunity to serve my Frozen Chocolate Delight. It is as delicious as it is beautiful.

Whether the dessert you long for is simple and light or rich and indulgent, this chapter offers the perfect—and perfectly delectable—finale to your meal.

Strawberry-Lemon Napoleons

These Napoleons are modern interpretations of a dessert classic. They are light, delicately flavored, and absolutely beautiful. You can use egg roll skins or phyllo pastry for the crisp layers.

1. Prepare the pudding according to package instructions. Set aside.

2. Heat the oil in a 12-inch skillet over medium heat. Add the egg roll skins, and lightly brown about 20 to 30 seconds on each side. Transfer the skins to a paper towel-lined plate. Lightly sprinkle with some of the granulated sugar.

3. In a medium-sized mixing bowl, add the strawberries, lemon juice, and the remaining sugar. Mix well.

4. To assemble each Napoleon, spoon 1 teaspoon of the pudding in the center of a dessert plate and top with an egg roll skin—sugar side up. (The pudding will act as "glue" to keep the stack from slipping on the plate.) Cover the egg roll skin with ¼ cup of strawberries, 3 tablespoons of the pudding, and another egg roll skin. Repeat the layers, ending with a third egg roll skin.

5. Sprinkle the top of the Napoleons and the plate with powdered sugar, and serve.

VEGAN CHOICE

- Use phyllo dough instead of egg roll skins. (Instructions for making phyllo squares are given in the Colorado Bean Stack recipe on page 146.)

- Use soy-based lemon pudding, or Soy Lemon Crème (page 186).

Yield: 4 servings

2 boxes (4 ounces each) instant lemon pudding, or 1½ cups Lemon Cream Sauce (page 186)

1 tablespoon canola oil

12 egg roll skins (4-inch squares)

½ cup granulated sugar

2 cups quartered fresh strawberries

4 teaspoons lemon juice

Powdered sugar for garnish

Banana Cream Stacks

Similar to the Strawberry-Lemon Napoleons (page 171), this banana dessert is sweetened with brown sugar and apricot jam.

Yield: 4 servings

2 boxes (4 ounces each) instant lemon pudding, or 1 1/2 cups Lemon Cream Sauce (page 186)

2 tablespoons canola oil

12 egg roll skins (4-inch squares)

1/2 cup brown sugar

1/2 cup apricot jam

1/2 cup water

4 medium-sized bananas, cut into 1/2-inch slices

Powdered sugar for garnish

1. Prepare the pudding according to package instructions. Set aside.

2. Heat the oil in a 12-inch skillet over medium heat. Add the egg roll skins, and lightly brown about 20 to 30 seconds on each side. Transfer the skins to a paper towel-lined plate.

3. Combine the brown sugar, jam, and water in a 2-quart saucepan, and place over medium heat. Stir well. Bring to a boil, then reduce the heat to low and simmer the mixture for about 3 minutes. Remove from the heat, cool for about 10 minutes, then add the bananas. Stir to coat the bananas well.

4. To assemble each stack, spoon 1 teaspoon of the pudding in the middle of a dessert plate and top with an egg roll skin. (The pudding will act as "glue" to keep the stack from slipping on the plate.) Cover the egg roll skin with 1/4 cup of the banana mixture, 1/4 cup of the pudding, and another egg roll skin. Repeat the layers, ending with a third egg roll skin.

5. Sprinkle the top of the stacks and the plate with powdered sugar, and serve.

VEGAN CHOICE

- Use phyllo dough instead of egg roll skins. (Instructions for making phyllo squares are given in the Colorado Bean Stack recipe on page 146.)
- Use soy-based lemon pudding, or Soy Lemon Crème (page 186).

Cranberry Sorbet

*I place a scoop of this refreshing sorbet on a bed of cranberry relish
and serve it as an intermezzo during Thanksgiving dinner.*

Yield: 6 cups

2 cups whole cranberries

2 cups sugar

½ teaspoon sea salt

4 cups orange juice

1. Place the cranberries, sugar, salt, and 2 cups of the orange juice in a blender, and blend until smooth.

2. Transfer the mixture to a 2-quart saucepan over medium heat, and bring to a boil. Remove from the heat, add the remaining 2 cups of orange juice, and mix well.

3. Pour the mixture into a flat plastic 2-quart container, and place in the freezer.

4. When the mixture is completely frozen, cut it with a sharp, sturdy knife into 1½-inch cubes. Place the cubes in a food processor, and process until completely pulverized.

5. Serve immediately, or place in a plastic container and return to the freezer until ready to use.

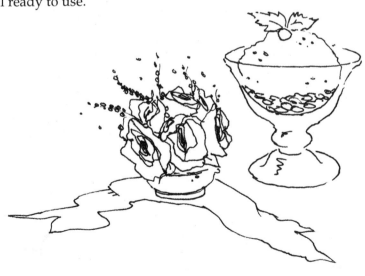

Basic Pie Crust

Light and flaky, this crust is the perfect foundation for pies, tarts, and quiches. I believe using butter in the dough is one of the keys to its success. Of course, proper preparation and baking techniques are important factors as well.

Yield: Two 9-inch crusts

³/₄ cup whole wheat pastry flour

³/₄ cup all-purpose white flour

¹/₄ cup cold butter

Pinch salt

2 teaspoons granulated sugar

¹/₂ cup ice water

1. In a large mixing bowl, combine the flours. Using a pastry blender or two knives, cut the butter into the flour until the mixture becomes a crumbly meal.

2. Stir the salt and sugar into the ice water and pour it over the flour mixture. Using a fork, mix the water with the flour mixture until the dough binds together. (If the dough appears too wet, add a little whole wheat flour.) Form the dough into two balls, and let rest a few minutes.

3. Turn one ball of dough onto a floured surface, and flatten it into a ¹/₂-inch-thick circle.

4. With a floured rolling pin, roll out the dough (from the center outward) to a 10-inch circle that is ¹/₈ to ¹/₁₆ inch thick. Transfer the dough to a 9-inch pie pan.

5. If using a single crust, crimp or flute the edge, and press it firmly against the sides of the pan. Add the filling and bake according to the specific recipe.

6. If the recipe calls for a top crust, roll out the second ball of dough as instructed above. Drape the top crust over the filling. Join the edges of the top and bottom crusts, roll up, and crimp. With a sharp knife, pierce the top crust in three or four places to allow steam to escape during baking.

VEGAN CHOICE

- Use corn oil in place of the butter.

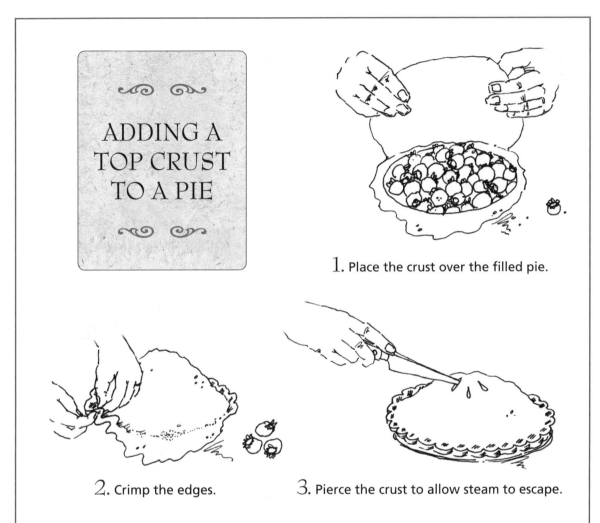

ADDING A TOP CRUST TO A PIE

1. Place the crust over the filled pie.

2. Crimp the edges.

3. Pierce the crust to allow steam to escape.

If you are prebaking a single crust, expect it to shrink and puff up as it bakes. To compensate for the shrinkage, before crimping the edges, lift the dough and gently nudge it toward the center of the pan. This will take away some of the tension. Also, leave 1/4- to 1/2-inch slack on the edges.

To eliminate or minimize the dough from puffing up as it bakes, poke holes in it with the tines of a fork before putting it in the oven. Or, you can place a pie pan of the same size on top of the crust before baking.

After the crust has been in the oven for 6 to 8 minutes, remove the pan and let the crust finish baking. At that point, it won't puff any more.

Always bake the crust in a preheated 400°F oven. The high heat is imperative for a flaky dough. The usual baking time is about 15 minutes, or until the crust is lightly browned. If the dough is still soft, it isn't ready. And although the baked crust will seem hard when it comes out of the oven, it will become tender and flaky as it sets.

Walnut Tart

Enjoy a slice of this sensational tart topped with a dollop of whipped cream. (Recipes for regular and vegan whipped creams are found on pages 188 and 187, respectively).

1. Preheat the oven to 275°F.

2. Place the walnuts in a food processor, and pulse until they are coarsely chopped. Increase the oven temperature to 350°F.

3. Transfer the nuts to a large mixing bowl, along with the corn syrup, sugar, arrowroot, and vanilla extract. Stir well.

4. Roll out half the dough to a ⅛-inch-thick, 13-inch circle. Place the dough in an 11-inch tart pan, pressing it gently on the bottom and up the sides (there should be some overlapping). Spoon the walnut filling on top.

5. Roll out the remaining dough for the top crust. Place it on top of the filling, letting the edges hang over the side of the pan. Brush the edges of the bottom crust with water, then join the edges of the top and bottom crusts and seal them together. Using a knife, cut a number of slits in the top crust to allow steam to escape as the tart bakes

6. Bake for 35 minutes, or until the crust is lightly browned. To give the top crust a rich brown color, brush it with a mixture of ¼ cup corn syrup and ¼ cup water during the last 4 or 5 minutes of baking.

7. Remove the tart and let it sit at least 20 minutes before cutting it into wedges and serving.

VEGAN CHOICE

• Use vegan pie crust. See the version on page 174.

Nancy's Peach Pie

I developed this recipe especially for my wife, Nancy.
Try it à la mode with your favorite ice cream.

1. Preheat the oven to 350°F.

2. In a mixing bowl, combine the peaches, sugar, arrowroot, lemon juice, cinnamon, mace, and salt. Mix well.

3. Roll out half of the dough into an 11-inch circle, and press it into the bottom of a 10-inch pie plate. Carefully pour the peach filling into the pan.

4. Roll out the remaining dough into another 11-inch circle, and drape it over the filling. Wet the edge of the bottom crust with water, then join the edges of the top and bottom crusts. Roll up and crimp. With a sharp knife, pierce the top crust in three or four places to allow steam to escape during baking.

5. Bake for 35 to 45 minutes, or until the crust is golden brown, and the filling is hot and bubbly.

6. Let cool to room temperature before cutting.

VEGAN CHOICE

- Use vegan pie crust. See the version on page 174.

Yield: 10-inch pie

6 cups sliced fresh or frozen peaches

½ cup brown sugar, or sucanat

3 tablespoons arrowroot powder

2 tablespoons lemon juice

¼ teaspoon ground cinnamon

⅛ teaspoon ground mace

⅛ teaspoon sea salt

1 recipe Basic Pie Crust (page 174)

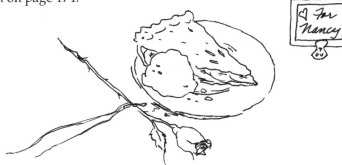

Pineapple Mango Pie

Pineapple and mango are two of my favorite tropical fruits,
which come together in this summer dessert.

Yield: 10-inch pie

Yield: 10-inch pie

5 tablespoons white flour

2 tablespoons granulated
sugar

¼ teaspoon sea salt

1 recipe Basic Pie Crust
(page 174)

2 cups peeled, sliced mangos

3 cups bite-sized
pineapple chunks

¼ cup coconut milk

1. Preheat the oven to 375°F.

2. In a small mixing bowl, combine the flour, sugar, and salt. Set aside.

3. Roll out half of the dough into an 11-inch circle, and press it into the bottom of a 10-inch pie plate. Layer the mangos evenly in the bottom of the pan, and sprinkle with half of the flour mixture. Top with a layer of pineapple, then sprinkle with the rest of the flour mixture. Drizzle the coconut milk over the top.

4. Roll out the remaining dough into an 11-inch circle, and drape it over the filling. Wet the edge of the bottom crust with water, then join the edges of the top and bottom crusts. Roll up and crimp. With a sharp knife, pierce the top crust in three or four places to allow steam to escape during baking.

5. Bake for 35 to 45 minutes, or until the crust is golden brown, and the filling is hot and bubbly.

6. Let cool to room temperature before cutting.

VEGAN CHOICE

• Use vegan pie crust. See the version on page 174.

Zuppa Inglese

This Italian parfait, literally translated as "English soup," is similar to the British trifle. Traditionally, it is made with rum-sprinkled slices of sponge cake that are nestled between layers of rich custard and candied fruit. I think you'll find this variation just as good.

1. Place the raspberries and kiwi in a bowl, add the anisette, and toss to coat. Set aside.

2. To assemble each parfait, place 1 tablespoon of pudding in the bottom of a parfait glass, and top with about 2 tablespoons chocolate cake crumbs. Next, add 4 tablespoons of raspberry/kiwi mixture, and top with ¼ cup pudding. Repeat. Drizzle any remaining anisette over the tops.

3. Serve immediately or chill before serving. Covered and refrigerated, these parfaits will keep up to five days.

VEGAN CHOICE

- Use vegan-style Coconut Pudding (page 183).

Yield: 4 servings

½ cup fresh raspberries, or chopped strawberries

½ cup peeled, diced kiwi

¼ cup anisette liqueur

2 cups Coconut Pudding (page 183), or 4-ounce box flavored pudding of choice, prepared

1 cup chocolate cake crumbs

Frozen Chocolate Delight

Calling all chocolate lovers! This special-occasion frozen chocolate cake is for you. It takes a fair amount of time to prepare, but is well worth the effort.

Yield: Double-layer 8-inch cake

1¼ cups whole wheat pastry flour

1 cup unbleached white flour

½ cup brown sugar

½ cup sifted cocoa powder

1 teaspoon baking soda

1 cup corn syrup

¾ cup whole milk

½ cup warm melted butter

1 large beaten egg

1 tablespoon cider vinegar

2 teaspoons vanilla extract

1 quart vanilla ice cream

½ cup nut butter of choice

1 recipe Chocolate Ganache (page 188), or other chocolate glaze

1. Preheat the oven to 350°F. Oil and flour two 8-inch cake pans.

2. In a medium-sized mixing bowl, combine the flours, brown sugar, cocoa powder, and baking soda. Mix well.

3. In a large mixing bowl, place the corn syrup, milk, melted butter, egg, vinegar, and vanilla extract, and mix well. This can be done either by hand or with an electric mixer.

4. Add the dry ingredients to the wet ingredients in ½-cup amounts. Beat well after each addition, until the batter is smooth. Evenly divide the batter between the two pans.

5. Bake for 20 minutes, or until a wooden toothpick inserted into the center of the cake comes out clean. Let the cakes cool to room temperature before removing them from the pans.

6. When completely cool, wrap the two cakes with plastic wrap and place them in the freezer for at least 1 hour, or until frozen. Line one of the cake pans with plastic wrap. (The wrap should hang over the sides of the pan.) Unwrap the frozen cakes and place one back in the pan.

7. Place the ice cream and nut butter in the bowl of an electric mixer with a paddle, and beat until slightly smooth but still frozen. Quickly spread the softened ice cream on the cake in the pan, then top with the remaining frozen cake layer. Cover with plastic wrap and immediately return it to the freezer.

8. Prepare the ganache. Remove the frozen cake from the freezer, and pour the ganache on top. Once again, return the cake (uncovered) immediately to the freezer. If you won't be serving the cake for a while, cover it after the ganache sets.

9. When ready to serve, carefully lift the cake out of the pan using the plastic wrap, and place it on a cake plate. Slice and serve. (For easy cutting, heat the knife by dipping it into hot water, then quickly wiping it dry.)

VEGAN CHOICE

- Use soy milk instead of whole milk.
- Replace the butter with canola oil.
- Replace the egg with 1 tablespoon flax meal.
- Use a soy-based vanilla ice cream instead of the dairy type.
- Use the vegan version of Chocolate Ganache (page 188).

Fresh Summer Fruit Salad

Enjoy this refreshing mélange of fruit, which is as beautiful as it is delicious, at any time of the day.

1. Place all of the ingredients except the mint in a large mixing bowl, and mix together well.

2. Sprinkle with mint, and serve immediately alongside a scoop of your favorite sorbet. You can also place the fruit in a covered container and refrigerate for a day or two.

Yield: 12 servings

4 cups watermelon, seeded and diced into bite-sized pieces

4 cups cantaloupe, seeded and diced into bite-sized pieces

3 cups stemmed, quartered strawberries

2 cups seedless dark grapes

1 cup $\frac{1}{4}$-inch kiwi slices

$\frac{1}{2}$ cup frozen lemonade concentrate

12 large mint leaves, chopped

Almond Crisp Cookies

*Try one of these crisp almond cookies
with a cup of your favorite tea.*

Yield:
About 16 cookies

2 cups whole wheat pastry flour

1/4 teaspoon sea salt

2 cups raw almonds

1 cup corn syrup

3/4 cup softened butter

1/2 teaspoon vanilla extract

1/8 teaspoon almond extract

16 whole almonds

1. Preheat the oven to 275°F. Combine the flour and salt in a mixing bowl, and set aside. Lightly oil a baking or cookie sheet.

2. Roast the almonds according to the instructions on page 52, and then allow them to cool for about 5 minutes. Increase the oven temperature to 325°F.

3. Place the almonds in a food processor, along with the corn syrup, butter, vanilla extract, and almond extract. Blend until smooth. Add the flour mixture and continue to mix about 30 seconds, or until a dough forms.

4. Roll 2-tablespoon portions of dough into balls and place them about 2 inches apart on the cookie sheet. Gently flatten each ball into a 1/4-inch thickness, and press a whole almond into the center of each.

5. Bake for 15 to 20 minutes, or until lightly browned. Remove from the oven, and cool the cookies on the tray for 1 minute. Transfer the cookies to a wire rack and cool completely. Serve immediately, or transfer to an airtight container.

VEGAN CHOICE

- Use corn oil instead of butter.

Coconut Pudding

If you're a fan of coconut, this is the pudding for you! Enjoy it as is, or use it as a pastry cream for a variety of desserts, especially Napoleons. It is also perfect for Zuppa Inglese on page 179.

1. Combine the coconut milk, whole milk, and sugar in a 2-quart saucepan. Place over medium heat, bring to boil while stirring, then reduce the heat to medium-low and simmer.

2. In a small mixing bowl, combine the water and arrowroot, and add it to the pan. Simmer, stirring constantly, for 4 to 7 minutes, or until the mixture thickens.

3. Remove from the heat, stir in the vanilla, and let cool. Spoon into individual pudding cups, cover with plastic wrap, and refrigerate.

4. Serve chilled.

Yield: 6 servings

1 cup coconut milk

2 cups whole milk

6 tablespoons granulated sugar

$\frac{1}{4}$ cup water

4 tablespoons arrowroot

$\frac{1}{2}$ teaspoon vanilla

VEGAN CHOICE

- Replace the whole milk with soy milk.

Chocolate Hazelnut Truffles

Imagine using leftover chocolate cake or brownies to create an elegant upscale dessert. Place these truffles on a tray and serve them with chocolate-covered strawberries and miniature pastries.

1. Preheat the oven to 275°F.

2. Roast the hazelnuts according to the instructions on page 52, and then allow them to cool for about 5 minutes. Place the nuts in a blender, and grind them to a medium-fine texture. Set aside.

3. Place the chocolate chips in a small saucepan over low heat, or in a double boiler set over boiling water. Stir constantly until they are completely melted. Remove the pan from the heat, and set aside.

4. In the bowl of an electric mixer, combine the cake crumbs, butter, and rum. Beat on medium speed for 3 to 5 minutes, or until smooth. Add the chocolate, and continue mixing another 3 minutes.

5. Form tablespoon-size portions of the mixture into balls. (If the mixture is too soft to form balls, let it sit for 30 to 60 minutes. This will allow the crumbs to absorb the moisture and for the chocolate to cool.) Roll the balls in the hazelnuts, then place them on a cookie sheet that is lined with wax paper.

6. Chill before serving.

VEGAN CHOICE

- Substitute hazelnut butter for the regular variety.

Apple Topping

Serve this nutty apple topping warm over ice cream,
or heated as a filling for crepes.

1. Preheat the oven to 275°F.

2. Roast the pecans according to the instructions on page 52, and then allow them to cool for about 5 minutes. Place the nuts in a blender, and grind them to a medium-coarse texture. Set aside.

3. Heat the butter in a 12-inch sauté pan over medium-low heat. Add the apples and sauté for 5 minutes, or until they are beginning to soften.

4. Add the nuts, brown sugar, rum, maple syrup, and lime juice, and stir well. Bring to a boil, then reduce the heat and simmer for 5 minutes, or until the apples are soft but firm, and the liquid has a sauce-like consistency.

5. Remove from the heat, and either use immediately, or store in a covered container in the refrigerator.

Yield: 2 cups

⅓ cup pecan halves

1 tablespoon butter

4 apples, peeled and cut into thick slices

¼ cup brown sugar

2 tablespoons rum

2 tablespoons maple syrup

1 tablespoon lime or lemon juice

VEGAN CHOICE

• Replace the butter with canola oil.

Lemon Cream Sauce

Not only is this thick lemon-kissed sauce a wonderful pastry cream, it makes a heavenly dip for fresh berries, kiwi, and mangos.

Yield: 3½ cups

1½ cups white chocolate chips

2 packages (12-ounces each) extra-firm silken tofu

Zest of 2 medium lemons (about 2 tablespoons)

2–3 drops natural yellow food color

1. Place the chocolate chips in a small saucepan over low heat, or in a double boiler set over boiling water. Stir constantly until they are completely melted. Remove the pan from the heat and set aside.

2. Place the tofu and zest in a blender and blend until smooth. Gradually add the melted chocolate and food coloring while the blender is running. Mix well.

3. Use immediately, or transfer the sauce to a covered container and refrigerate until ready to use. It will keep in the refrigerator up to 2 weeks.

Soy Lemon Crème

This creamy lemon sauce is very easy to prepare.

Yield: 3½ cups

12-ounce package extra-firm silken tofu

½ cup raw macadamia nuts

½ cup granulated sugar

¼ cup water

Zest of 1 medium lemon (about 1 tablespoon)

1. Place all of the ingredients in a blender, and blend until smooth.

2. Use immediately, or transfer the sauce to a covered container and refrigerate until ready to use. It will keep in the refrigerator up to 2 weeks.

Tofu Cream

*This is a rich cream with all of the body and flavor
of regular whipped cream.*

1. Place all of the ingredients in a blender, and blend until smooth.

2. Use immediately, or transfer to a covered container and refrigerate. It will keep for 10 to 14 days.

Yield: 3 cups

12-ounce package silken tofu

1 cup canola oil

$\frac{1}{2}$ cup soy milk powder

$\frac{1}{2}$ cup granulated sugar

2 teaspoons vanilla extract

$\frac{1}{4}$ cup cold water

Quick Raspberry Sauce

*This sauce is delicately sweet and intensely raspberry.
Try it with just about any chocolate dessert,
such as the Frozen Chocolate Delight on page 180.*

1. Place all of the ingredients in a 1-quart saucepan over medium heat. Stir to combine while bringing to a boil.

2. Remove from the heat, and either use immediately, or store in a covered container in the refrigerator.

Yield: $\frac{1}{2}$ cup

$\frac{1}{4}$ cup seedless raspberry jam

$\frac{1}{4}$ cup clear corn syrup

1 tablespoon lemon juice

Whipped Cream

Using cold whipping cream will ensure a firm final product.
For a vegan version, try the Tofu Cream on page 187.

Yield: 3 cups

2 cups whipping cream

¾ cup granulated sugar

2 teaspoons vanilla extract

1. Place all ingredients in a large mixing bowl, and whip with a hand-held electric mixer until smooth and firm.

2. Use immediately, or transfer to a covered container and refrigerate. It will keep for 5 to 7 days.

Chocolate Ganache

This rich dark-chocolate blend is typically used as a glaze for
cakes. It can also be beaten until fluffy, and used as a
base for truffles or other chocolate confections.

Yield: 1½ cups

4 tablespoons butter

½ cup milk

1 teaspoon vanilla extract

1½ cups bittersweet chocolate chips

1. Place the butter, milk, and vanilla in a 2-quart saucepan over medium heat, or in a double boiler set over boiling water. Heat thoroughly, and add the chocolate chips. Stir gently until the chips have melted and the sauce is well blended and has the consistency of thick cream.

2. To use as a cake glaze, pour the warm ganache over a cake that is placed on a wire rack and set over a baking sheet. Spread the ganache with a spatula. It will run down the sides of the cake and onto the baking sheet.

3. If not using immediately, transfer the ganache to a covered container and refrigerate, where it will keep for about 3 weeks. Rewarm in a double boiler before using.

VEGAN CHOICE

- Instead of butter, use 1 tablespoon canola oil.
- Use soy milk instead of whole milk.

Metric Conversion Tables

Common Liquid Conversions

Measurement	=	Milliliters
$1/4$ teaspoon	=	1.25 milliliters
$1/2$ teaspoon	=	2.50 milliliters
$3/4$ teaspoon	=	3.75 milliliters
1 teaspoon	=	5.00 milliliters
$1^1/4$ teaspoons	=	6.25 milliliters
$1^1/2$ teaspoons	=	7.50 milliliters
$1^3/4$ teaspoons	=	8.75 milliliters
2 teaspoons	=	10.0 milliliters
1 tablespoon	=	15.0 milliliters
2 tablespoons	=	30.0 milliliters

Measurement	=	Liters
$1/4$ cup	=	0.06 liters
$1/2$ cup	=	0.12 liters
$3/4$ cup	=	0.18 liters
1 cup	=	0.24 liters
$1^1/4$ cups	=	0.30 liters
$1^1/2$ cups	=	0.36 liters
2 cups	=	0.48 liters
$2^1/2$ cups	=	0.60 liters
3 cups	=	0.72 liters
$3^1/2$ cups	=	0.84 liters
4 cups	=	0.96 liters
$4^1/2$ cups	=	1.08 liters
5 cups	=	1.20 liters
$5^1/2$ cups	=	1.32 liters

Conversion Formulas

LIQUID		
When You Know	Multiply By	To Determine
teaspoons	5.0	milliliters
tablespoons	15.0	milliliters
fluid ounces	30.0	milliliters
cups	0.24	liters
pints	0.47	liters
quarts	0.95	liters

WEIGHT		
When You Know	Multiply By	To Determine
ounces	28.0	grams
pounds	0.45	kilograms

Converting Fahrenheit to Celsius

Fahrenheit	=	Celsius
200–205	=	95
220–225	=	105
245–250	=	120
275	=	135
300–305	=	150
325–330	=	165
345–350	=	175
370–375	=	190
400–405	=	205
425–430	=	220
445–450	=	230
470–475	=	245
500	=	260

Resources

The following companies, which are all well established with strong national and/or regional distribution, offer many of the high-quality vegetarian/vegan foods that are called for in this book. The majority of these products are readily available in most major supermarkets, health food stores, and gourmet shops. If, however, you are unable to find a particular item, contact the company, which can either sell you the desired product directly or inform you of a nearby store that carries it. It is also recommended that you visit the company websites, if one is available.

Arrowhead Mills, Inc.
PO Box 2059
Hereford, TX 79045
806–364–0730

Arrowhead Mills produces and distributes organically grown whole grains, flours, beans, nut butters, and cereals.

Devansoy Farms
PO Box 885
Carroll, IA 51401
800–747–8605
www.devansoy.com

Devansoy sells high-quality powdered soy milk in original and vanilla flavors.

Eco-Cuisine, Inc.
PO Box 17878
Boulder, CO 80308–0878
303–402–0289
www.ecocuisine.com

Eco-Cuisine's products include a line of Quick-Mix meat analogs, which are fast and easy to prepare. It also offers a variety of mixes for baked goods, such as cookies, brownies, and breads—all are vegan, and include recipe variations for adding eggs and dairy if preferred. Eco-Cuisine develops products for the food service industry and private labels, both nationally and internationally.

Ener-G Foods, Inc.
PO Box 84487
Seattle, WA 98124–5787
206–767–6600
800–331–5222
www.ener-g.com

In addition to its full line of wheat- and gluten-free products, Ener-G Foods sells Egg Replacer, an egg substitute that is made primarily of potato and tapioca starch. This product is free of wheat, gluten, dairy, egg, sugar, yeast, salt, and soy. Visit the Ener-G Foods website to find quality baked goods, cereals, and more for people with special dietary needs.

Frontier Natural Products Co-op
PO Box 299
Norway, IA 52318
800–669–3275
800–786–1388
www.frontiercoop.com

Frontier's Herb and Spice Collection includes an array of organic herbs, spices, and spice blends, as well as lecithin granules.

Galaxy Foods/Soyco
2441 Viscount Row
Orlando, FL 32809
800–441–9419
800–808–2325
407–855–7485 (fax)
www.galaxyfoods.com

Galaxy sells a line of Veggie brand soy casein and plant-based soy cheeses, which are available in a variety of flavors.

Harvest Direct, Inc.
PO Box 50906
Knoxville, TN 37950–0906
800–838–2727
865–539–2737 (fax)
www.harvestdirect.com

Harvest Direct is a developer, manufacturer, and distributor of textured soy products, which come in dry form and are easy to prepare. It offers a line of poultry, beef, pork, and seafood analogs; dairy alternatives; and Seitan Quick Mix. Harvest Direct also offers dry broth bases, including vegetarian beef, chicken, and ham flavored varieties.

Lightlife Foods, Inc.
153 Industrial Boulevard
Turners Falls, MA 01376
800–274–6001
www.lightlife.com

Lightlife offers an excellent line of seitan and tempeh products, breakfast meat alternatives, soy cold cuts, and a line of vegetarian-style burgers, hot dogs, and sausages. Both frozen and ready-to-eat refrigerated products are readily available.

The Mail Order Catalog for Healthy Eating
413 Farm Road
Box 180
Summertown, TN 38483
800–695–2241
931–964–2291 (fax)
www.healthy-eating.com

This mail order company offers vegetarian products from a number of companies listed in this Resources section, including both Eco-Cuisine and Harvest Direct. Toll-free ordering is available 24 hours a day, 7 days a week.

Morinaga Nutritional Foods, Inc.
2050 West 190th Street,
Suite 110
Torrance, CA 90504
800–669–8638
www.morinu.com

In addition to its line of Mori-Nu silken tofu products—including "lite" varieties—Morinaga also offers tofu pudding mixes.

Mountain Ark Trading Company
799 Old Leicester Highway
Asheville, NC 28806
800–643–8909
www.mountainark.com

Mountain Ark imports and distributes a variety of natural foods, including sea vegetables, regular and specialty grains and pastas, miso, tamari, shoyu, mirin, and specialty vinegars.

Omega Nutrition USA, Inc.
6505 Aldrich Road
Bellingham, WA 98226
800–661–3529
www.omeganutrition.com

Omega sells a variety of high-quality unrefined oils, which are primarily, if not completely, organic. In addition to sesame and olive oils, the company offers flax seed oil and such specialty oils as hazelnut. To protect them from light, which hastens deterioration, the oils are packaged in distinctive black bottles.

P.J. Lisac & Associates, Inc.
9001 SE Lawnfield Road
Clackamas, OR 97015
503–652–1988
www.lisanatti.com

Lisac's Lisanatti brand cheeses are high in calcium, low in sodium, and made from expeller-pressed canola oil and either organic rice, soy milk, or almond milk. As they are also made with casein, these cheeses are not totally plant based. They are, however, cholesterol, lactose, and preservative free.

Turtle Mountain, Inc.
PO Box 70
Junction City, OR 97448
541–998–6778
541–998–6344 (fax)
www.turtlemountain.com

Turtle Mountain sells Soy Delicious—a line of all-natural, organic dairy-free frozen desserts.

Vogue Cuisine, Inc.
3710 Grandview Boulevard
Los Angeles, CA 90066
888–236–4144
www.voguecuisine.com

Vogue Cuisine sells a line of high-quality, low-sodium bases, including VegeBase (a blend of specially prepared soybeans and dehydrated vegetables), Onion Base, Beef Base, and Chicken Base.

White Wave
1990 North 57th Court
Boulder, CO 80301
303–443–3470
www.whitewave.com

White Wave produces and sells a line of high-quality soyfoods, including Silk soymilk, tofu, baked tofu, tempeh, and ready-to-eat seitan.

Yves Veggie Cuisine, Inc.
1638 Derwent Way
Delta, BC V3M 6R9
Canada
800–667–9837
www.yvesveggie.com

Yves Veggie Cuisine produces an excellent line of vegetarian meats, including veggie dogs, burgers, deli slices, breakfast meats, entrées, and veggie cheeses. All products are sold in the produce/deli section of your supermarket. The website can guide you to a local store that carries the Yves Veggie Cuisine line.

About the Author

Ron Pickarski is the first professional vegetarian chef to be certified as an Executive Chef (CEC) by the American Culinary Federation. A recognized expert in the preparation of both traditional and vegetarian cuisine, Mr. Pickarski, also known as Chef Ron, is the president and the executive research and development chef of Eco-Cuisine, Inc., a food technology consulting service. There, he has helped develop several food-product lines. After becoming the first professional chef to win a medal for vegan cuisine at the prestigious Culinary Olympics in 1980, Chef Ron and his American Natural Foods Team went on to win a total of seven medals to date. He also gives educational demonstrations and food seminars for foodservice professionals, and is the author of *Friendly Foods* and *Eco-Cuisine: An Ecological Approach to Gourmet Vegetarian Cooking.*

Index